Differentiating Instruction With Menus

Geometry

ADVANCED-LEVEL MENUS
Grades 9–12

Differentiating Instruction With Menus

Geometry

Laurie E. Westphal, Ed.D.

PRUFROCK PRESS INC.
WACO, TEXAS

Prufrock Press Inc.
P.O. Box 8813
Waco, TX 76714-8813
Phone: (800) 998-2208
Fax: (800) 240-0333
http://www.prufrock.com

CONTENTS

PART I

All About Menus and Choice

CHAPTER 1

Choice

"For so many reasons, it is simply the right thing to do for this age group."

—Shared by a group of secondary teachers when asked why choice is important for their students

Why Is Choice Important?

Ask any adult if he or she would prefer to choose what to do or be told what to do, and of course, he or she is going to prefer the choice. Students, especially teenagers, have these same feelings. Although they may not always stand up and demand a choice if none are present, they benefit in many ways from having them.

One benefit of choice is its ability to meet the needs of so many different students and their varied learning preferences. The Dunedin College of Education (Keen, 2001) conducted a research study on the preferred learning styles of 250 gifted students. Students were asked to rank different learning options. Of the 13 different options described to the students, only one option did not receive at least one negative response, and that was choice. Although all students have different preferences, choice is the one option that meets all students' needs. Why? Well, it takes the focus from the teacher as the decision maker and allows students to decide what is best for them. What teenager would argue against being able to do something that he or she prefers to do? When given the opportunity to choose, students are going to choose what best fits their educational needs.

"I really was not sure how my students were going to react to these choices. I didn't want the menu to be viewed as busy work when we already had so much content to cover. I was surprised (and relieved) by how well they responded [to the choices]. Now, they want to have choice in everything, which is always up for negotiation."

—English II teacher

Another benefit of choice is its ability to address different learning preferences and ultimately offer the opportunity to better assess what students understand about the content being studied. During professional development, I often ask teachers what learning preferences are most addressed in the products they provide. Not surprisingly, visual and written products top the list. These two preferences are most popular for many reasons, including ease of grading, ease of organizing and managing, and lack of supplies needed. In looking back on all of the different products my students have created, however, I noticed that most often, the tactile, kinesthetic, and verbal products provided greater depth and complexity (Komarraju, Karau, Schmeck, & Avdic, 2011). After analyzing these "noisy" products, I have come to realize that if I really want to know what my students understand, I need to allow them to show me through their learning preference—and the most common preferences of my students are not visual-written. Most students prefer tactile-kinesthetic (Dunn & Honigsfeld, 2013; Ricca, 1984; Sagan, 2010; Snyder, 1999). Because these preferences are not always addressed during whole-class instruction, teachers need a strategy that can allow students to express themselves. Using choice to offer these opportunities can help address the needs of more students in our classrooms.

Another advantage of choice is a greater sense of independence for the students (Deci, Vallerand, Pelletier, & Ryan, 1991; Patall, 2013; Robinson, Patall, & Cooper, 2008). When teachers offer choice, students design and create a product based on what they envision, rather than what their teacher envisions. When students would enter my classroom, many times they had been trained by previous teachers to produce what the teacher wanted, not what the students thought would be best. Teaching my students that what they envision could be correct (and wonderful) could be a struggle. "Is this what you want?" or "Is this right?" were popular questions as we started the school year. As we progressed, and I continued to redirect their questions back to them ("Is that what you would like to show?" or "Does that seem right to you?"), students began to ask for my approval less; they became more independent in their work. They might still need assurance, but the phrasing was different, "This is what I have so far. Can I ask for help from Joe?" or "I don't like this; I am going to pick something else." When teachers allow students choice in the products they create to show their learning, the students can develop this independence.

Increased student focus and persistence is another benefit of offering choice. When students are making choices in the activities they wish to complete, they are more focused on the learning that is needed to create their choice products (Flowerday & Schraw, 2003; Ricca, 1984). Students become engaged when they learn information that can help them develop products that they are excited about creating. Many students struggle with the purpose of the information being taught in the classroom, and this can lead to behavior problems. Students may feel disconnected from the content and lose interest (Robinson et al., 2008). Instead, students will pay closer attention to instruction when an immediate application (the student's choice product) for the knowledge being presented in class is present. If students are excited about the product, they are more focused on the content; they are less likely to be off task during instruction.

Many a great educator has referred to the idea that the best learning takes place when the students have a desire to learn. Some students have a desire to learn anything that is new to them; others do not want to learn anything unless it has interest for them. By incorporating choice activities that require the students to stretch beyond what they already know, teachers create a void which needs to be filled. This void leads to a desire to learn.

A Point to Ponder: Making Good Choices Is a Skill

"I want my students to be independent, and it can be frustrating that they just can't make decisions for themselves. I hadn't thought I might need to actually teach decision-making skills."

—Secondary study skills teacher, after hearing me discuss choice as a skill

When we think of making a good choice as a skill, much like writing an effective paragraph or essay, it becomes easy enough to understand that we need to encourage students to make their own choices. In keeping with this analogy, students could certainly figure out how to write on their own, and perhaps even how to compose sentences and paragraphs, by modeling other examples. Imagine, however, the progress and strength of the writing produced when students are given guidance and even the most basic of instruction on how to accomplish the task. The written piece is still their own, but the quality of the finished piece is much stronger when guidance is given during the process. There is a reason why class time is spent in the AP classroom focusing on how to write an appropriate response to a document-based question (DBQ) or free-response question (FRQ). Students need to practice the skill before the big test in May. The same is true with choices; the quality of choices our high school students can make in the classroom is directly impacted by exposure and practice.

As with writing, students could make choices on their own, but when the teacher provides background knowledge and assistance, the choices become more meaningful and the products richer. All students certainly need guidance (even if our strong-willed high school students think they know it all), as the idea of choice may be new to them. Some students may only have experienced basic instructional choices, like choosing between two journal prompts or perhaps having the option of making either a poster or a PowerPoint presentation about the content being studied. Some may not have experienced even this level of choice. This lack of experience can cause frustration for both teacher and student.

Teaching Choices as a Skill

So, what is the best way to provide guidance and enable our students to develop the skill of making good choices while still allowing them to develop their individuality? First, choose the appropriate number of choices for your students. Although the goal might be to have students choose from 20 different options, teachers might start by having their students choose from three predetermined choices the first day (if they were using a game show menu, for instance, students might choose an activity from the first column). Then, after that product had been created, students could choose from another three options from another column a few days later, and perhaps from another three the following week. By breaking students' choices down, teachers reinforce how to approach or attack a more complex and/or varied choice format in the future. All students can work up to making complex choices from longer lists of options as their choice skill level increases.

Second, although our high school students feel they know everything now, they may still need guidance on how to select the option that is right for them. They may not automatically gravitate toward options without an exciting and detailed description of each choice. For the most part, students have been trained to produce what the teacher requests, which means that when given a choice, they may choose what seems to be the easiest and what the teacher most wants (then they can get to what they would prefer to be doing). This means that when the teacher discusses the different menu options, he or she must be equally as excited about each option. The discussion of the different choices must be somewhat animated and specific. For example, if the content is all very similar, the focus should be on the product: "If you want to create something you might see on YouTube, this one is for you!" or "If you want to be artistic, check this one as a maybe!" The more exposure students have to the processing the teacher provides, the more skillful they become in their choice making.

How Can Teachers Allow Choice?

"The GT students seem to get more involved in assignments when they have choice. They have so many creative ideas and the menus give them the opportunity to use them."

—Secondary social studies teacher, when asked about how students respond to having choices

When people visit a restaurant, they are all attending with the common goal of finding something on the menu to satisfy their hunger. We all hope that when students come into our classroom, they will have a hunger as well—a hunger for learning. Choice menus are a way of allowing students to choose how they would like to satisfy that hunger. At the very least, a menu is a list of choices that students use to choose an activity (or activities) they would like to complete to show their learning. At best, it is a complex system in which students are given point goals and complete different products to earn points (which are based on the levels of Bloom's revised taxonomy; Anderson & Krathwohl, 2001). These menus should have a way to incorporate a "free-choice" option for those picky eaters who would like to make a special order to satisfy their learning hunger.

The next few sections provide examples of different menu formats that will be used in this book. Each menu has benefits, limitations or drawbacks, and time considerations. An explanation of the free-choice option and its management will follow the information on each type of menu.

Tic-Tac-Toe Menu

"My students really enjoy the Tic-Tac-Toe menus, and I get them to stretch themselves without them realizing it."

— High school AP World Geography teacher

Description

The Tic-Tac-Toe menu (see Figure 1.1) is a well-known, commonly used menu that contains a total of eight predetermined choices and one free choice for students. These choices can range from task statements leading to product creation, complex and/or higher level processing questions, or leveled problems for solving. The choices can be created at the same level of Bloom's revised taxonomy or can be arranged in such a way to allow for the three different levels or objectives within a unit or topic. If all choices have been created at the same level of Bloom's revised taxonomy, then each choice carries the same weight for grading and has similar expectations for completion time and effort.

Benefits

Flexibility. This menu can cover either one topic in depth, three different topics, or three objectives within one content area. When this menu covers just one objective, and all tasks are from the same level of Bloom's revised taxonomy (preferably the highest), students have the option of completing three projects in a tic-tac-toe pattern, or simply picking three from the menu. When the menu covers three objectives, three different levels of Bloom's revised taxonomy, or three different learning preferences, students will need to complete a vertical or horizontal tic-tac-toe pattern only (either a vertical column or horizontal row) to be sure they have completed one activity from each objective, level, and learning style.

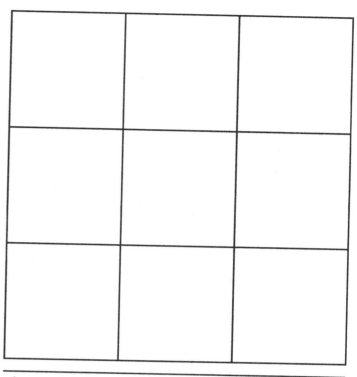

Figure 1.1. Tic-Tac-Toe menu example.

Stretching. When students make choices on this menu by completing a row or column based on its design, they will usually face one choice that is out of their comfort zone. This "stretch" may result from a task's level of Bloom's revised taxonomy, its product style, or its content. Students will complete this "uncomfortable" choice because they want to do the other two in that row or column.

Friendly design. Students quickly understand how to use this menu. It is nonthreatening because it does not contain points, and therefore it seems to encourage students to stretch out of their comfort zones.

Weighting. All products are equally weighted, so recording grades and maintaining paperwork are easily accomplished.

Short time period. They are intended for shorter periods of time, between 1–3 weeks based on the tasks found on the menu as well as the amount of class time allotted for students to work on the menu.

Limitations

Few topics. These menus only cover one or three topics.

Student compromise. Although this menu does allow choice, when following the guidelines of rows or columns only, the menu provides only six different ways to meet the goal. This restriction means a student will sometimes have to compromise and complete an activity he or she would not have chosen because it completes his or her tic-tac-toe. (This is not always bad, though!)

No "safety net." Because each product in this menu is recorded as its own grade, it is possible that a student could fail this menu. Other formats allow students to make a poor choice and still earn full credit by completing additional options.

Time Considerations

Tic-Tac-Toe menus usually are intended for shorter amounts of completion time—at the most, they could take up to 3 weeks with students working outside of class and submitting one product each week. If a menu focuses on one topic in-depth and the students have time in class to work on their products, the menu could be completed in one week.

Meal Menu

"Seemed pretty easy at first—after all it was only three things and I was thinking I would just have to draw a few equations. All the lunch and dinner real world stuff was hard— [I] had to really think."

—High school Algebra II student

Description

The Meal menu (see Figure 1.2) is a menu with a total of at least nine predetermined choices as well as two or more enrichment/optional activities for students. The choices are created at the various levels of Bloom's revised taxonomy and incorporate different learning preferences, with the levels getting progressively higher and more complex as students progress from breakfast to lunch and then dinner. All products carry the same weight for grading and have similar expectations for completion time and effort. The enrichment or optional (dessert) options can be used for extra credit or replace another meal option at the teacher's discretion.

Benefits

Great starter menu. This menu is very straightforward and easy to understand, so time is saved in presenting the completion expectations.

Flexibility. This menu can cover either one topic in depth or three different objectives or aspects within a topic, with each meal representing a different aspect. With this menu, students have the option of completing three products: one from each meal.

Optional enrichment. Although not required, the dessert category of the Meal menu allows students to have the option of going further or deeper if time during the unit permits. This option could also be used, at teacher discretion, as a replacement of low score on one of the meal products.

Chunkability. The Meal menu is very easy to break apart into smaller pieces. Whether you have students who need support in making choices or you only want to focus on one aspect of a topic at a time, this menu can accommodate these decisions. Students could be asked to select a breakfast while the rest of the menu is put on hold until the breakfast product is submitted, then a lunch product is selected, and so on.

Friendly design. Students quickly understand how to use this menu because of its real-world application.

Weighting. All products are equally weighted, so recording grades and maintaining paperwork are easily accomplished with this menu.

Short time period. Meal menus are intended for shorter periods of time, between 1–3 weeks.

Breakfast
☐ _____
☐ _____
☐ _____

Lunch
☐ _____
☐ _____
☐ _____

Dinner
☐ _____
☐ _____
☐ _____

Dessert
☐ _____
☐ _____

Figure 1.2. Meal menu example.

Limitations

No "safety net." Because each product in this menu is recorded as its own grade, it is possible that a student could fail this menu, unless the teacher allows the optional dessert to replace a low grade on one of the meal products.

Time Considerations

Meal menus usually are intended for shorter amounts of completion time—at the most, they should take 3 weeks with students working outside of class and submitting one product each week. If the menu focuses on one topic in-depth and the students have time in class to work on their products, the menu could be completed in one week.

List Menu/"Challenge List"

"Of the different formats I tried this year, I really liked the challenge list format. I could modify the menu simply by changing the [point] goal. When I had a student test out of two days, I simply upped [his or her] goal to 140, and [he or she] worked on [his or her] menu during instructional time. It was a huge success!"

—Secondary math teacher

Description

The basic List menu (see Figure 1.3), or Challenge List, has a total of at least 10 predetermined choices, each with its own point value, and at least one free choice for students. Choices are simply listed with assigned points based on the levels of Bloom's revised taxonomy. The choices carry different weights and have different expectations for completion time and effort. A point criterion is set forth that equals 100%, and students choose how they wish to attain that point goal. There are different versions of the list menu included in this book: the Challenge List (one topic in depth) and a Multitopic List Menu (which, based on its structure, can accommodate more than one topic).

Benefits

Grade-as-you-go. This menu requires that teachers grade products as the students complete them. Actively grading and providing immediate feedback are important so the students can alter their plans and choose to submit additional products to be sure they reach the point goal. Additionally, by grading-as-you-go, teachers will not have piles of products to grade once the menu is completed.

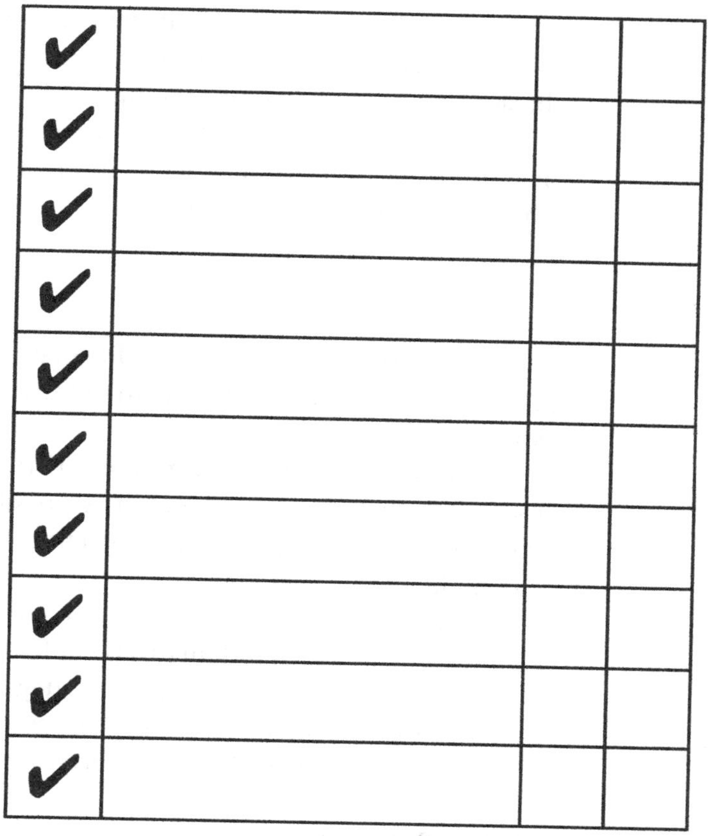

Responsibility. Students have complete control over their grades. Students like the idea that they can guarantee their grade if they complete their required work and meet the expectations outlined in the rubric and product guidelines. If students do not earn full credit on one of the chosen products, they can complete another product to be sure they have met their point goal. This responsibility over their own grades also allows a shift in thinking about grades—whereas many students think of grades in terms of how the teacher judged their work, or what the teacher "gave me," having control over their grades leads students to understand that they earn their grades.

Figure 1.3. List menu example.

Different learning levels. This menu has the flexibility to allow for individualized contracts for different learning levels within the classroom. Because classrooms may have many ability levels, it might be necessary to contract students based on their ability or results from the pretesting of content. In which case, each student can contract for a certain number of points for his or her 100%.

Concept reinforcement. This menu allows for an in-depth study of the material. With the different levels of Bloom's revised taxonomy being represented, however, students who are at the early stages of learning the concepts can choose lower-level point value products to reinforce the basics before jumping into the higher level activities.

Variety. A list menu offers a larger variety of product choices. There is guaranteed to be a product of interest to everyone. (And if there isn't, there is always free choice!)

Limitations

One topic. If using the traditional challenge list format, this menu can only be used for one topic in depth, so that students cannot miss any specific content.

Cannot guarantee objectives. If the traditional challenge menu is used for more than one topic, it is possible for a student to not have to complete an activity for each objective, depending on the choices he or she makes.

Preparation. Teachers need to have all materials ready at the beginning of the unit for students to be able to choose any of the activities on the list. This expectation requires a degree of advanced planning. (*Note*: This advanced preparation leads to low stress during the unit as all of the materials have already been gathered.)

Time Considerations

List menus usually are intended for shorter amounts of completion time—at the most, 2 weeks. (*Note*: Once you have assembled the materials, the preparation is minimal!)

20-50-80 Menus

As you suggested, I used one of your 20-50-80 menus as homework to review equations of a line the week before we went into solving systems of equations. It was very easy for the students to understand and saved so much time at the beginning of the systems unit. I am going to use these more often.

—Algebra I teacher

Description

A 20-50-80 menu (see Figure 1.4; Magner, 2000), is a variation on a List menu, with a total of at least eight predetermined choices: no more than two choices with a point value of 20, at least four choices with a point value of 50, and at least two choices with a point value of 80. Choices are assigned these points based on the levels of Bloom's revised taxonomy. Choices with a point value of 20 represent the remember and understand levels, choices with a point value of 50 represent the apply and analyze levels, and choices with a point value of 80 represent the evaluate and create levels. All levels of choices carry different weights and have different expectations for completion time and effort. Students are expected to earn 100 points for a 100%. Students choose what combination of products they would like to complete to attain that point goal.

Figure 1.4. 20-50-80 menu example.

Benefits

Responsibility. With this menu, students have complete control over goals and their grade. (*Note*: This is not to say that it is acceptable for students to choose 70% as their goal. The expectation is always that the students will work to achieve or exceed the point goal for the menu.)

Guaranteed activity. This menu's design is set up in such a way that students must complete at least one activity at a higher level of Bloom's revised taxonomy to reach their point goal.

Grade-as-you-go. This menu requires that teachers grade products as the students complete them. Actively grading and providing immediate feedback are important so the students can alter their plans and choose to submit additional products to be sure they reach the point goal. Additionally, by grading-as-you-go, teachers will not have piles of products to grade once the menu is completed.

Low stress. This menu is one of the shortest menus. If students choose well and complete quality products, they could accomplish their goal by completing just two products. This menu is usually not as daunting as some of the longer, more complex menus. The 20-50-80 menu provides students a great introduction into the process of making choices.

Limitations

One topic. If this menu is used for more than one topic, it is possible for a student to not have to complete an activity for each objective, depending on the choices he or she makes. Therefore, a 20-50-80 menu is limited in the number of topics it can assess.

Limited higher level thinking. Students could potentially complete only one activity at a higher level of thinking (although many students will complete more to allow themselves a "cushion" in case they do not earn full credit on a product.

Time Considerations

These menus are usually intended for a shorter amount of completion time—at the most, 2 weeks with students working outside of class, or one week, if class time is allowed for product completion.

Game Show Menu

"It was different, doing a [game show] menu. I had to really consider how I was going to get enough points but still do all the topics. By the time I was done, at least I know I got a 100% on a major grade."

—High school U.S. history student

Description

The Game Show menu (see Figure 1.5) is a complex menu. It can cover multiple topics or objectives with three predetermined choices and a free student choice for each objective. Choices are assigned points based on the levels of Bloom's revised taxonomy. All choices carry different weights and have different expectations for completion time and effort. A point criterion is set forth that equals 100%. Students must complete at least one activity from each objective to reach their goal.

Benefits

Free choice. This menu allows the most free-choice options of any of the menu formats. Although it has many choices for students, if they do not want to complete the offered activities, students can propose their activity for each objective addressed on the menu.

Responsibility. This menu allows students to guarantee their grade as long as they meet the point goal for 100%.

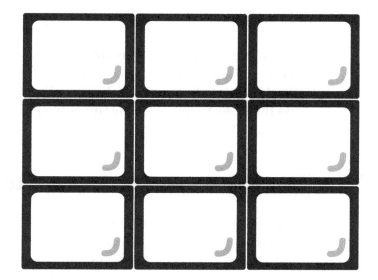

Figure 1.5. Game Show menu example.

Grade-as-you-go. This menu requires that teachers grade products as the students complete them. By grading-as-you-go, teachers will not have piles of products to grade once the menu is completed.

Different learning levels. The game show menu has the flexibility to allow for individualized contracts for different learning levels within the classroom. Each student can create a contract for a certain number of points for his or her 100%.

Objectives guaranteed. The teacher is guaranteed that the students complete an activity from each objective covered, even if it is at a lower level.

Limitations

Confirm expectations. The only real limitation of the Game Show menu is that students (and parents) must understand the guidelines for completing the menu. Teachers need to remember to copy the instruction page on the back of the menu!

Time Considerations

These menus usually are intended to be completed in a longer amount of time. Although teachers could use these menus yearlong (each column could be a grading period), they usually are intended for 2–3 weeks based on the tasks found on the menu as well as the amount of class time allotted for students to work on the menu.

Free Choice

"I try to bring in real-world applications for each concept we cover. Sometimes it might be the students simply answering, 'How does this apply to your life?' So, now I let them use the free-choice proposals and they can create something to show me the application of the material."

—High school AP Chemistry teacher

As a menu option, students may be offered the opportunity to submit a free choice for their teacher's consideration. Figure 1.6 shows two sample proposal forms that have been used many times successfully in my classroom. The form provided to students is based on the type of menu being presented. If using a target-based menu like the Tic-Tac-Toe or Meal menu, there is no need to submit a free-choice proposal form that includes the mention of points.

When implementing a menu that includes free choice, a copy of the appropriate free-choice proposal form should be given to each student when the menu is first introduced. The form should be discussed with the students, so they understand the expectations of proposing a free choice. If they do not want to make a proposal after you have discussed the menu and its activities, the students can place unused forms in a designated place. I always had a box of blank proposal forms on the supply table in my classroom, so unused forms could be returned there. Some students may want to keep their free-choice proposal form "just in case"—you may be surprised who wants to submit a proposal form after hearing about the opportunity!

These proposal forms must be submitted before students begin working on their free choice. That way, the teacher knows what the students are working on, and the student knows the expectations for the product

Name: _____ **Teacher's Approval:** _____

Free-Choice Proposal Form for Point-Based Menu

Points Requested:		Points Approved:	

Proposal Outline

1. What specific topic or idea will you learn about?

2. What criteria should be used to grade it? (Neatness, content, creativity, artistic value, etc.)

3. What will your product look like?

4. What materials will you need from the teacher to create this product?

Name: _____ **Teacher's Approval:** _____

Free-Choice Proposal Form for Menus

Proposal Outline

1. What specific topic or idea will you learn about?

2. What criteria should be used to grade it? (Neatness, content, creativity, artistic value, etc.)

3. What will your product look like?

4. What materials will you need from the teacher to create this product?

Figure 1.6. Free-choice proposal forms.

of choice. Once approved, the forms can be stapled to the student's menu sheet for reference. The students can refer to it as they develop their free choice, and when the grading takes place, the teacher can refer to the agreement for the "graded" features of the product.

Each part of the proposal form is important and needs to be discussed with students during the introductory discussion of the form.

- *Name/Teacher's approval.* It is very important that the student submits this form to the teacher. The teacher will carefully review all of the information, give it back to the student for clarification if needed, and then sign the top. Although not always possible, I preferred that the students discuss their forms with me, so we can both be clear about their ideas.

- *Points requested.* Only on the point-based menu proposal form, this is usually where negotiation takes place. Students will often submit their first free-choice request for a very high number of points (even the 100% goal). Students tend to equate the amount of time an activity or product will take with the amount of points it should earn. Unfortunately, the points are always based on the level of Bloom's taxonomy. A PowerPoint with a vocabulary word quiz would get minimal points although it may have taken a long time to create. If the students have not been exposed to the levels of Bloom's taxonomy, the assigning of points can be difficult to explain. Teachers can always refer to the popular "Bloom's Verbs" to help explain the different between time and higher level activities.

- *Points approved.* Only on the point-based menu proposal form, this is the final decision recorded by the teacher once the point haggling is finished.

- *Proposal outline.* This is where the students will tell you everything about the product that they intend to complete. These questions should be completed in such a way that you can picture what they are planning on completing. These questions also show you that the students know what they are planning on completing as well.
  - *What specific topic or idea will you learn about?* Students need to be specific here, not just "science" or "writing." This response is where the students need look at the objectives or standards of the unit and choose which objective they would like to address through their product.

o *What criteria should be used to grade it?* Although there are guidelines for all of the projects that the students might create, it is important for the students to explain what criteria are most important in its evaluation. The student may indicate that the product guideline being used for all of the predetermined product is fine; however, they may also want to add other criteria here.

o *What will your product look like?* It is important that this response be as detailed as possible. If students cannot express what it will "look like," then they have probably not given their free choice enough thought.

o *What materials will you need from the teacher to create this product?* This question is an important consideration. Sometimes students do not have the means to purchase items for their project. These materials can be negotiated as well, but if you ask what students may need, they often will develop even grander ideas for their free choice. This may also be a place for students to note any special equipment or technology needs they may have to create their product.

CHAPTER 2

How to Use Menus in the Classroom

Instructional menus can be used in different ways in the secondary classroom. To decide how to implement your choice menu, the following questions should be considered:

- How confident are your students in making choices and working independently?
- How much intellectually appropriate information is readily available for students to obtain on their own?
- How much prior knowledge of the topic being taught do the students have before the unit or lesson begins?

After considering the responses to these questions, there is a variety of ways to use menus.

Building Background Knowledge or Accessing Prior Knowledge

"I have students with so many different experiences—sometimes I spend a lot more time than I allotted to review and get everyone up to speed before we get started."

—Secondary social studies teacher

There are many ways to use menus in the classroom. One way that is often overlooked is using menus to review or build background knowledge or access prior knowledge before a unit begins. Using menus this way is beneficial when students have had exposure to upcoming content in the past, perhaps during the previous year's instruction or through life experiences. Many high school students have had preliminary exposure to the basic information needed in their classes. However, students may not remember the details of the content at the depth needed to proceed with the upcoming unit immediately. A shorter menu covering the background or previous year's objectives can be provided the week prior to the new unit. This way, students have the opportunity to recall and engage with the information in a meaningful way, while not using valuable class time during the first day of a new unit to do so. Because the teacher knows that the students have covered the content in the past, the students should be able to work independently on the menu by engaging their prior knowledge. Students work on products from the selected menu as anchor activities and/or homework throughout the week preceding the new unit, with all products being submitted prior to the upcoming unit's initiation. By using menus in this manner, students have been thinking about the upcoming unit for a week and are ready to investigate the topic further. Students are prepared to take their knowledge to a deeper level on the first day of instruction, conserving that much-needed instruction time.

Enrichment and Supplemental Activities

"Just because my students are teenagers doesn't mean they do not need enrichment; the problem is finding time. My curriculum is so packed, and I had always had trouble getting any in. I tried using an enrichment menu for the body systems since I thought we might have enough time. The students really enjoyed it; they seemed to make time for it. I need to use more."

—High school biology teacher

Using menus for enrichment and supplementary activities is the most common way of implementing menus in the classroom. Many teachers who want to "dip their toes" in the menu pool will begin by using menus this way because it does not directly impact their current teaching style. The students usually do not have much background knowledge, and information about the topic may not be readily available to all students while working on the menu.

When using menus for enrichment or supplemental activities, the teacher should introduce the menu and the choice activities at the beginning of a unit—before any instruction has taken place. The teacher then will progress through the content at the normal rate using his or her curricular materials, periodically allowing class and/or homework time throughout the unit for students to work on their menu choices to supplement a deeper understanding of the lessons being taught. Although it may seem counterintuitive to provide enrichment before any instruction takes place, it actually facilitates a need to know, or an epistemic curiosity (Litman, 2005).

This method incorporates an immediate use for the content the teacher is providing. For example, at the beginning of a unit, the teacher introduces the menu with the explanation that students may not have all of the knowledge to complete their choices yet. As instruction progresses, however, more content will be provided, and the students will be prepared to work on new choices. If students want to work ahead, they certainly can find the information on their own, but this is not required. Gifted students often see the ability to work ahead as a challenge and will begin to investigate concepts mentioned in the menu before the teacher has discussed them. Other students may start to develop questions about the concepts and then are ready to ask their questions when the teacher covers the new material. This "advance investigation" helps build an immense pool of background knowledge and potential content questions before the topic is even discussed in the classroom. As teachers, we constantly fight the battle of having students read ahead or "come to class prepared for discussion." By introducing a menu at the beginning of a unit and allowing students to complete products as instruction progresses, we encourage the students to naturally investigate the information and come to class prepared without having to make preparation a separate requirement.

Mainstream Instructional/Flipped Classroom Activities

"On your suggestion, I tried using the Game Show menu with my geometry unit since I had 3 days of instruction that the students knew well and could work on independently. They really responded to the independence."

—Secondary math teacher

Another option for using menus in the classroom is to offer a choice between certain in-class curricular activities. For example, after students have obtained basic instruction outside of the classroom (through research, videos, or other sources), students can be offered a menu of choices to organize their activities and facilitate their learning during class time. The students spend class time working on the activities on their menus; the teacher spends class time facilitating the choices that students have selected.

If teachers follow a more traditional model, menus can be used when students have some limited background knowledge about the content and appropriate information is readily available for them among their classroom resources. The teacher would select which aspects of the content must be directly taught to the students and which could be appropriately learned and reinforced through product menu activities. The unit is then designed using both formal instructional lessons and specific menu days during which the students will use the menu to strengthen the prior knowledge they already have learned, apply the new information, or extend recently presented information in a differentiated way. For this use of menus to be effective, the teacher must feel very comfortable with the students' prior knowledge level and their readiness to work independently.

Mini-Lessons

"I have so many different levels in my classroom, using menus with mini-lessons has been a life saver. I actually can work with small groups and everyone else doesn't run wild!"

—Secondary math teacher

Another option for menu use is the use of mini-lessons, with the menus driving the accompanying classroom activities. This method is best when most of the students have similar degrees of knowledge about the topic. The teacher designs short 10–15-minute mini-lessons, in which students quickly review fundamental concepts that already are familiar to them as well as experience new content in a brief, concise way. After these short mini-lessons, students can select an activity on the menu to demonstrate their understanding of the new concept.

The Game Show menu usually works well with mini-lessons. The menu can be designed so the topics across the top of the menu represent one mini-lesson per day (column). Using menus in this way shortens the amount of time teachers use the guided practice aspect of the lesson, so all instruction and examples should be carefully selected. The benefit of using menus with mini-lessons is the teacher gets to avoid the one-size-fits-all independent practice portion of the lesson. If a few students still struggle after the mini-lesson, they can be pulled into a small group while the other students work on their choices from the menu.

An important consideration when using menus this way is the independence level of the students. For mini-lesson menus to be effective, students will need to be able to work independently for up to 30 minutes after the mini-lesson. Students are often interested in the product they have chosen, so this may not be a critical issue, but it is still one worth mentioning as teachers consider how they would like to use various menus in their classroom.

CHAPTER 3

Guidelines for Products

"It was different being able to do something other than a drawing or folded paper. I haven't made a video for school in years!"

—High school chemistry student

This chapter outlines the different types of products used in the included menus as well as guidelines and expectations for each. It is crucial that students know the expectations of a product before they choose to work on it. By discussing these expectations before the students begin and having the information readily available, you will save frustration on everyone's part.

$1 Contract

"I really appreciate the $1 form. It kept me from having to run to [craft store] and spend $60 on felt and glitter and all of the other things we normally have to buy for projects."

—Parent of one of my students when asked for feedback on a recent menu

Consideration should be given to the cost of creating the products in any menu. The resources available to students vary within a classroom, and students should not be evaluated on the amount of materials they can purchase to make a product look glittery. The menus in this book are designed to equalize the resources students have available. For most products, the materials are available for under a dollar and can often be found in a teacher's classroom as part of his or her supplies. If a product would require materials from the student, the $1 contract is included as part of the product's guideline. This contract is an important aspect of the explanation of the product. By limiting the amount of money a child can spend, it creates an equality of resources for all students. This limitation also encourages a more creative product. When students are limited by the amount of materials they can readily purchase, they often have to use materials from home in new and unique ways. Figure 3.1 is a sample $1 contract that I have used many times with various products.

The Products

Table 3.1 contains a list of the products used in this book. These products were chosen for their flexibility in meeting learning preferences as well as being popular products most students have experienced and teachers may already use in their classroom. They have been arranged by learning preference—visual, kinesthetic, or auditory.

Each menu has been designed to include products from all of the learning preferences. Some of the products may be listed under more than one area depending on how they are presented or implemented (and some of the best products cross over between areas). The specific expectations (guidelines) for all of the products are presented in an easy-to-read card format that can be reproduced for students. This format is convenient for students to have in front of them when they work on their projects.

Product Frustrations

"One of the biggest reasons I haven't used more than one product at a time is that I have to constantly reexplain what I want for it. Even if the students write it down, it doesn't mean they won't pester me about it all week."

—English I teacher

$1 Contract

I did not spend more than $1.00 on my _____ .

_____   _____
Student Signature   Date

My child, _____ , did not spend more than $1.00
on the product he or she created.

_____   _____
Parent Signature   Date

Figure 3.1. $1 contract.

One of the biggest frustrations that accompany the use of a variety of menu products is the barrage of questions about the products themselves. Students can become so engulfed in the products and the criteria for creating them that they do not focus on the content being synthesized. This focus on products is especially true when menus are introduced to students.

Students can spend an exorbitant amount of time asking the teacher about the products mentioned on the menu. When this interrogation begins, what should have been a 10–15-minute menu introduction turns into 45–50 minutes of discussion about product expectations—without any discussion of the content!

During this discussion, teachers may consider showing students examples of the product(s) from the previous year. Although this can be helpful, it can also lead to additional frustration on the part of both the teacher and the students. Some students may not feel that they can produce a product as nice, as big, as special, or as (you fill in the blank) as the example. Alternatively, when shown an example, students might interpret that the teacher would like something exactly like the example he or she showed to students. To avoid this situation, I would propose that when using examples, students are shown a "blank" example that demonstrates how to create the shell of the product. For example, if a window pane is needed, students might be shown a blank piece of paper that the teacher has divided into six panes. The students can then take

Table 3.1
Products

Visual	Kinesthetic	Auditory/Oral
Acrostic	Board Game	Board Game
Advertisement	Book Cover	Children's Book
Book Cover	Bulletin Board Display	Class Game
Brochure/Pamphlet	Card Sort	Classroom Model
Cartoon/Comic Strip	Class Game	Commercial
Children's Book	Classroom Model	Game Show
Choose Your Own	Collage	Interview
Adventure	Commercial	News Report
Collage	Concentration Cards	Play
Crossword Puzzle	Diorama	Presentation of Created
Diary/Journal	Flipbook	Product
Drawing	Folded Quiz Book	PowerPoint–Speaker
E-mail	Game Show	Puppet Show
Folded Quiz Book	Mobile	Speech
Graphic Novel	Model	Song/Rap
Greeting Card	Mural	Student-Taught Lesson
Instruction Card	Museum Exhibit	You Be the Person
Letter	Play	Presentation
Map	Product Cube	Video
Mind Map	Puppet	
Newspaper Article	Quiz Board	
Poster	Scrapbook	
PowerPoint–Stand	Science Experiment	
Alone	Student-Taught Lesson	
Questionnaire	Three-Dimensional	
Quiz	Timeline	
Recipe	Trading Cards	
Scrapbook	Trophy	
Social Media Profile	Video	
Story	WebQuest	
Trading Cards		
Three Facts and a Fib		
Venn Diagram		
WebQuest		
Window Pane		
Worksheet		

the "skeleton" of the product and make it their own as they create their version of the window pane using their information.

Product Guidelines

"Wow. You know how great these are . . . how much time they will save?"

—A group of teachers, when presented with a page of products guidelines for their classroom

Most frustrations associated with the varied products placed on menus can be addressed proactively using standardized, predetermined product guidelines. These guidelines should be shared with students prior to them creating any products. Although these guidelines may look like "mini-rubrics," they are designed in a generic way, such that any time throughout the school year that students select a product, that product's guidelines will apply.

A beneficial side effect of using set guidelines for a product is the security the guideline creates in the choice-making process. Students are often reticent to try something new, as doing so requires taking a risk. Traditionally, when students select products, they ask questions about creating the product, hope they remember all of the details, and submit the product for grading. It can be quite a shock when the students receive the product back and realize that their product was not complete or was not what the teacher expected. As you can imagine, students may not want to take the risk on something new the next time. Instead, they may prefer to stick to what they know and be successful. Using standardized product guidelines, students can begin to feel secure in their choice before they start working on a new product. Without this security, students tend to stay within their comfort zone.

Sharing the Product Guidelines

"Wow! It's already done for us."

—A group of teachers at staff development after
discovering the product guidelines pages

The guidelines for all of the products used on the menus in this book, as well as some potential free-choice options, are included in an easy-to-read card format (see Figure 3.2). Once the topic menu has been selected, there are many ways to share this information with students. There is no one "right way" to share the product guideline information with your students. The method you select depends on your students' abilities and needs.

For students who are independent and responsible (yes, they do exist!), teachers may duplicate and distribute all of the product guidelines pages to students at the beginning of the year. Students can glue them into the front of their notebooks or punch holes and place them in binders. By providing them in advance, each student has his or her copy to use while working on menu products during the school year.

If teachers prefer a more controlled method, class sets can be created. These sets can be created by gluing each product guideline onto a separate index card, hole punching the corner of each card, and placing all of the cards on a metal ring. These ring sets can be put in a central location or at a supply table where students can borrow and return them as they work on their products. Using a ring also allows for the addition of products as they are introduced. Additionally, the rings and index cards can be color-coded based on learning preference, encouraging students to step out of their comfort zone during free choice.

Some teachers prefer to expose students to products as students experience them on their menus. In this case, product guidelines from the menu currently assigned can be enlarged and posted on a bulletin board or wall for easy access during classroom work. Some teachers may choose to reproduce each menu's specific product guidelines on the back of the menu.

No matter which method teachers select to share the product guideline information with the students, teachers will save themselves a lot of time and frustration by having the product guidelines available for student reference (e.g., "Look at your product guidelines—I think that will answer your question").

Acrostic	Advertisement	Board Game
• Must be at least 8.5" by 11" • Must be neatly written or typed • Target word must be written down the left side of the paper • Each descriptive phrase chosen must begin with one of the letters from the target word • Each descriptive phrase chosen must be related to the target word • Name must be written on the acrostic	• Must be at least 8.5" by 11" • Must include a meaningful slogan • Must include a color picture of item or service • Must include price, if appropriate • Could be developed electronically • Name must be written on the advertisement	• Must have at least four thematic game pieces • Must have at least 25 colored/thematic squares • Must have at least 20 question/activity cards • Must have thematic title on the game • Must have a complete set of rules for playing the game • Must be at least the size of an open file folder • Name must be written on the front of the board game

Book Cover	Brochure/Pamphlet	Bulletin Board Display
Must include five parts: • **Front cover**—title, author, image • **Cover inside flap**—paragraph summary of the book • **Back inside flap**—brief biography of author with at least five details • **Back cover**—editorial comments about book • **Spine**—title and author » May be placed on actual book, but not necessary » Name must be written on the book cover	• Must be at least 8.5" by 11" • Must be in three-fold format • Front fold must have the title and picture • Must have both pictures and information • Information must be in paragraph form with at least five facts included • Bibliography or sources must be provided if needed • Can be created on computer • Any pictures from the Internet must have proper credit • Name must be written on the cover of the brochure	• Must fit within assigned space on bulletin board or wall • Must include at least 10 details • Must have a title • Must have at least five different elements (posters, papers, questions, etc.) • Must have at least one interactive element that engages the reader • Name must be written on the bottom of the display

Card Sort	Cartoon/Comic Strip	Children's Book
• Must have at least 16 total cards • Must have at least five cards in each column • Can have more than two columns if appropriate • Answer key must be submitted • All cards must be submitted in a carrying bag • Name must be written on the carrying bag	• Must be at least 8.5" by 11" • Must have at least six cells • Must have meaningful dialogue that addresses the task • Must have color • Name must be written on the bottom of the cartoon or comic strip	• Must have a cover with book's title and student's name as author • Must have at least 10 pages • Each page must have an illustration to accompany the story • Must be neatly written or typed • Can be developed on the computer

Figure 3.2. Product guidelines.

Choose Your Own Adventure	Class Game	Classroom Model
• Must be neatly written or typed • Can be presented in an electronic format • Reader must be able to transition smoothly between choices • Readers must experience at least four choices in each story "strand" • Must include at least six unique endings • Must be appropriate length to allow for all of the adventures	• Game must allow all class members to participate • Must have only a few, easy-to-understand rules • Must be inventive or a new variation on a current game • Must have multiple question opportunities • Must provide answer key before the game is played • Name must be written on the answer key • The game must be approved by the teacher before being scheduled for play	• Must use everyone in the class in the model • Must not take longer than 2 minutes to arrange everyone • Students must be able to understand the part they play in the model • After the model is created, the explanation of the model must not take longer than 2 minutes • Must submit a paragraph that shares how the arrangement of students represents the concept being modeled • Name must be written on the paragraph submitted
Collage	**Commercial/Infomercial**	**Concentration Cards**
• Must be at least 8.5" by 11" • Pictures must be neatly cut from magazines or newspapers (no clip art) • Must label items as required in task • Name must be written on the bottom of the collage	• Must be between 1 and 3 minutes • Script must be turned in before commercial is presented • May be either live or recorded beforehand based on teacher discretion • Must have props or some form of costume(s) • Can include more than one person • Name must be written on the script	• Must have at least 20 index cards (10 matching sets) • Can use both pictures and words • Information must be placed on just one side of each card • Must include an answer key that shows the matches • All cards must be submitted in a carrying bag • Name must be written on the carrying bag
Cross Cut Model/Diagram	**Crossword Puzzle**	**Diary/Journal**
• Must include a scale to show the relationship between product and the actual item • Must include details about each layer • If creating a model, must also meet the criteria of a model • If creating a diagram, must also meet the criteria of a poster • Name must be written on the model	• Must have at least 20 significant words or phrases included • Clues must be appropriate • Must include puzzle and answer key • Can be created using a computer • Name must be written on the crossword puzzle	• Must be neatly written or typed • Must include the appropriate number of entries • Must include a date for each entry if appropriate • Must be written in first person • Name must be written on the diary or journal

Figure 3.2. Continued.

© Prufrock Press Inc. • *Differentiating Instruction With Menus: Geometry* • *Grades 9–12*

Diorama

- Must be at least 4" by 5" by 8"
- Must be self-standing
- All interior space must be covered with relevant pictures and information
- Name must be written on the back in permanent ink
- Must submit a signed $1 contract
- Informational/title card must be attached to diorama

Drawing

- Must be at least 8.5" by 11"
- Must show what is requested in the task statement
- Must include color
- Must be neatly drawn by hand
- Must have title
- Name must be written on the back

E-mail

- Must be neatly written or typed
- Must cover the specific topic of the task
- Must include standard to, from, and subject
- Must include appropriate (but fictitious) e-mail addresses of sender and recipient
- Must be signed with custom signature from sender

Essay

- Must be neatly written or typed
- Must cover the specific topic in detail
- Must be at least three paragraphs
- Must include bibliography or sources if appropriate
- Name must be written in the heading of the essay

Flipbook

- Must be at least 8.5" by 11" folded in half
- All information or opinions must be supported by facts
- Must be created with the correct number of flaps cut into the top
- Color is optional
- Name must be written on the back of the flipbook

Folded Quiz Book

- Must be at least 8.5" by 11"
- Must have at least 10 questions
- Must be created with the correct number of flaps cut into the top
- Questions must be written or typed neatly on upper flaps
- Answers must be written or typed neatly inside each flap
- Color is optional
- Name must be written on the back of the quiz book

Game Show

- Must have an emcee or host
- Must have at least two contestants
- Must have at least one regular round and a bonus round
- Questions must be content specific
- Props can be used, but are not mandatory
- Name must be written on the questions used in the game

Greeting Card

Must include four parts:
- **Front**—colored pictures, words optional
- **Front inside**—personal note related to topic
- **Back inside**—greeting or saying, must meet menu task
- **Back outside**—logo, publisher, and price for card
  - » Name must be written on the back of the card

Instruction Card

- Must be no larger than 5" by 8"
- Must be created on heavy paper or card
- Must be neatly written or typed
- Must use color drawings
- Must provide instructions stated in the task
- Name must be written on the back of the card

Figure 3.2. Continued.

Interview	Letter	Map
• Must have at least eight questions important to the topic being studied • Person chosen for interview must be an "expert" and qualified to provide answers based on product criteria • Questions and answers must be neatly written or typed • Name must be written on the interview questions	• Must be neatly written or typed • Must use proper letter format • Must have at least three paragraphs • Must follow type of letter stated in the menu (friendly, persuasive, informational) • Name must be included in the letter in a meaningful way	• Must be at least 8.5" by 11" • Must contain accurate information • Must include at least 10 relevant locations • Must include compass rose, legend, scale, key • Name must be written on the back of the map

Mind Map	Mobile	Model
• Must be at least 8.5" by 11" • Must use unlined paper • Must have one central idea • Must follow the "no more than four rule": There must be no more than four words coming from any one word • Must be neatly written or developed using a computer program • Name must be written on the mind map	• Must contain at least 10 pieces of related information • Must include color and pictures • Must include at least three layers of hanging information • Must be able to hang in a balanced way • Name must be written on one of the cards hanging from the mobile	• Must be at least 8" by 8" by 12" • Parts of model must be labeled • Must be in scale when appropriate • Must include a title card • Name must be permanently written on model

Mural	Museum Exhibit	News Report
• Must be at least 22" x 54" • Must have at least five pieces of important information • Must have colored pictures • Words are optional, but must have title • Name must be written on the back of the mural in a permanent way	• Must have title for exhibit • Must include at least five "artifacts" • Each artifact must be labeled with a neatly written card • Exhibit must fit within the size assigned • Must submit a signed $1 contract • No expensive or irreplaceable objects may be used in the display • Name must be written on a label card in the exhibit	• Must address the who, what, where, when, why, and how of the topic • Script of news report must be turned in with product, or before if performance will be "live" • May be either live or recorded beforehand based on teacher discretion • Name announced during the performance and clearly written on script

Figure 3.2. Continued.

Newspaper Article	Play/Skit	Poster
• Must be informational in nature • Must follow standard newspaper format • Must include picture with caption that supports article • Must contain at least three paragraphs • Must be neatly written or typed • Name must be written at the top of the article	• Must be between 3 and 5 minutes • Script must be turned in before play is presented • May be presented to an audience or recorded for future showing to audience based on teacher discretion • Must have props or some form of costume • Can include more than one person • Name must be written on the script that is submitted with the play	• Must be the size of a standard poster board • Must contain at least five pieces of important information • Must have title • Must have both words and pictures • Name must be written on the back of the poster in a permanent way • Bibliography or sources must be included as needed
PowerPoint–Stand Alone	**PowerPoint–Speaker**	**Project Cube**
• Must contain at least 10 informational slides • Must not have more than 10 words per page • Slides must have color and no more than one graphic per page • Animations are optional but must not distract from the information being presented • Bibliography or sources must be included as needed • Name must be written on the first slide of the PowerPoint	• Must contain at least 10 informational slides • Must not have more than two words per page • Slides must have color and no more than one graphic per page • Animations are optional but must not distract from information being presented • Presentation must be timed and flow with the speech being given • Name must be written on the first slide of the PowerPoint	• All six sides of the cube must be filled with information as stated in the task • Must be neatly written or typed • Name must be printed neatly on the bottom of one of the sides of the cube • Must be submitted flat for grading
Puppet	**Questionnaire**	**Quiz**
• Puppet must be handmade and must have a movable mouth • A list of supplies used to make the puppet must be turned in with the puppet • Must submit a signed $1 contract • If used in a puppet show, all play criteria must be met as well • Name must be written on the inside of the puppet where it can be seen	• Must be neatly written or typed • Must contain at least 10 questions with possible answers • Must contain at least one answer that requires a written response • Questions must be helpful to gathering information on the topic begin studied • If questionnaire is to be used, at least 15 people must provide answers • Name must be written at the top of the questionnaire	• Must be at least a half sheet of paper • Must be neatly written or typed • Must cover the specific topic in detail • Must include at least five questions, including at least one short answer question • Must have at least one graphic • An answer key must be turned in with the quiz • Name must be written on the top of the quiz

Figure 3.2. Continued.

Quiz Board

- Must have at least five questions
- Must have at least five answers, although there could be more for distractors
- Must use a system with lights to facilitate self-checking
- Name must be written in a permanent way on the back of the quiz board

Recipe/Recipe Card

- Must be written neatly or typed on a piece of paper or an index card
- Must have a list of ingredients with measurements for each
- Must have numbered steps that explain how to make the recipe
- Name must be written at the top of the recipe card

Scrapbook

- Cover of scrapbook must have a meaningful title and student's name
- Must have at least five themed pages
- Each page must have at least one meaningful picture
- All photos and pictures must have captions
- Bibliography or sources must be included as needed

Social Media Profile

- Must include profile picture
- Must include other relevant information about the "person"
- Must include at least five status updates with comments from "friends"
- Can be created electronically or in poster format
- Name must be included on the social media profile in a creative way

Song/Rap

- Must be original (not found online or sung by anyone else before)
- Words or lyrics must make sense
- May be either live or recorded beforehand based on teacher discretion
- Written words must be turned in before performance or with taped song
- Must be at least 2 minutes in length
- Name must be written on the written words submitted with the song or rap

Speech

- Must be at least 2 minutes in length
- Must not be read from written paper
- Note cards can be used
- Written speech must be turned in before speech is presented
- May be either live or recorded beforehand based on teacher discretion
- Voice must be clear, loud, and easy to understand
- Name must be written on the written speech

Story

- Must be neatly written or typed
- Must have all elements of a well-written story (setting, characters, conflict, rising action, and resolution)
- Must be appropriate length to allow for story elements
- Name must be written on the story

Three-Dimensional Timeline

- Must not be bigger than a standard-size poster board
- Must be divided into equal time units
- Must contain at least 10 important dates
- Must have at least two sentences explaining why each date is important
- Must have a meaningful object securely attached beside each date to represent that date
- Objects must be creative
- Must be able to explain how each object represents each date or event
- Name must be written at the bottom of the timeline

Three Facts and a Fib

- Can be handwritten, typed, or created in PowerPoint
- Must include exactly four statements: three true statements (facts) and one false statement (fib)
- False statement must not be obvious
- Brief paragraph must accompany product that explains why the fib is false
- Name must be written on the product

Figure 3.2. Continued.

Trading Cards	Trophy	Venn Diagram
• Must include at least 10 cards • Each card must be at least 3" by 5" • Each card must have a colored picture • Must contain at least three facts on the subject of the card • Cards must have information on both sides • All cards must be submitted in a carrying bag • Name must be written on the carrying bag	• Must be at least 6" tall • Must have a base with the name of the person getting the trophy and the name of the award written neatly or typed on it • Top of trophy must be appropriate and represent the nature of the award • Name must be written on the bottom of the award • Must be an original trophy (avoid reusing a trophy from home)	• Must be at least 8.5" by 11" • Diagram shapes must be thematic (rather than just circles) and neatly drawn • Must have a title for entire diagram and a title for each section • Must have at least six items in each section of the diagram • Name must be written neatly on the back of the paper
Video	**WebQuest**	**Window Pane**
• Must use video format • Must submit a written plan or story board with project • Students must arrange their own way to record their video or allow teacher **at least** 3 days notice for help in obtaining a way to record the video • Must cover pertinent information • Name must be written on the label or in the file name	• Must quest through at least five high-quality websites • Websites must be linked in the document • Can be submitted using a word processor or PowerPoint • Must contain at least three questions for each website • Must address the topic • Name must be written on the WebQuest or in the file name	• Must be at least 8.5" by 11" on unlined paper • Must contain at least six squares • Each square must include both a picture and words • All pictures must be both creative and meaningful • Must be neatly written or typed • Name must be written on the bottom right hand corner of the front of the window pane
Worksheet	**You Be the Person Presentation**	
• Must be 8.5" by 11" • Must be neatly written or typed • Must cover the specific topic or question in detail • Must be creative in design • Must have at least one graphic • An answer key must be turned in with the worksheet • Name must be written at the top of the worksheet	• Presenter must take on the role of the person • Must cover at least five important facts about the life or achievements of the person • Must be between 2 and 4 minutes in length • Script must be turned in before information is presented • Must be presented to an audience with the ability to answer questions while in character • Must have props or some form of costume • Name must be written on the script	

Figure 3.2. Continued.

CHAPTER 4

Rubrics

"One rubric—and I can grade everything? Now we are talking!"

—Group of secondary teachers

The most common reason teachers feel uncomfortable with menus is the need for fair and equal grading. If all of the students create the same product, teachers feel these products are easier to grade than 100 different products, none of which looks like any other. The great equalizer for hundreds of different products is a generic rubric that can evaluate the important qualities of an excellent product.

All-Purpose Rubric

Figure 4.1 is an example of a rubric that has been classroom tested with various menus. This rubric can be used with any point value activity presented in a menu, as there are five criteria, and the columns represent full points, half points, and no points. For example, if a student completes a 20-point product, each criterion would be worth four points (full

All-Purpose Rubric

Name: _____

Criteria	Excellent (Full Credit)	Good (Half Credit)	Poor (No Credit)	Self
Content Is the content of the product well chosen?	Content chosen represents the best choice for the product. Information or graphics are well chosen and related to content.	Information or graphics are related to content, but are not the best choice for the product.	Information or graphics present do not appear related to the topic or task.	
Completeness Is everything included in the product?	All information needed is included. Product meets the product guideline criteria and the criteria of the menu task.	Some important information is missing. Product meets the product guideline criteria and the criteria of the menu task.	Most important information is missing. The product does not meet the task or does not meet the product criteria.	
Creativity Is the product original?	Presentation of information is from a new and original perspective. Graphics are original. Product includes elements of fun and interest.	Presentation of information is from a new perspective. Graphics are not original. Product has elements of fun and interest.	There is no evidence of new thoughts or perspectives in the product, or any part of the product was plagiarized.	
Correctness Is all of the information included correct?	All information presented is correct and accurate.		Any portion of the information presented in product is incorrect.	
Communication Is the information in the product well communicated?	All information is neat and easy to read. Product is in appropriate format and shows significant effort. Oral presentation was easy to understand and presented with fluency.	Most (80%) of the product is neat and easy to read. Product is in appropriate format and shows significant effort. Oral presentation was easy to understand, with some fluency.	More than 20% of the product is not neat and easy to read, or the product is not in the appropriate format. It does not show significant effort. Oral presentation was not fluent or easy to understand.	
			Total Grade:	

Figure 4.1. All-purpose rubric.

points), two points (half points), and zero (no points). Although Tic-Tac-Toe and Meal menus are not point based, this rubric can also be used to grade products from these menus. Teachers simply assign 100 points to each of the three products on the Tic-Tac-Toe and Meal menus. Then each criterion would be worth 20 points, and the all-purpose rubric can be used to grade each product individually.

There are different ways that teachers can share this rubric with students. Some teachers prefer to provide it when they present a menu to students. The rubric can be reproduced on the back of the menu along with its guidelines. The rubric can also be given to students at the beginning of the year with the product guideline cards. This way, students will always know the expectations as they complete projects throughout the school year. Some teachers prefer to keep a master copy of the rubric for themselves and post an enlarged copy on a bulletin board. If teachers wanted to share the rubric with parents, they could provide a copy for parents during back-to-school night, open house, or on private teacher web pages so that the parents will understand how teachers will grade their children's products.

No matter how teachers choose to share the rubric with students, the first time students see this rubric, it should be explained in detail, especially the last column, titled "Self." It is imperative that students self-evaluate their products. The Self column can provide a unique perspective on the product as it is being graded. *Note*: This rubric was designed to be specific enough that students will understand the criteria the teacher is seeking, but general enough that they can still be as creative as they like in the creation of their product.

Student-Taught Lessons and Oral Presentations

Although the all-purpose rubric can be used for all of the activities included on the menus in this book, there are two occasions that seem to warrant a special rubric: student-taught lessons and oral presentations. These are unique situations, with many fine details that must be considered to create a quality product.

Although valuable for both the student "teachers" and those in audience, student-taught lessons are not commonly used in the geometry classroom. Secondary math curriculum is already packed with information, and turning class time over to students should only be done if it will benefit everyone involved; therefore, it can cause stress for both students and teachers. Teachers often would like to allow students to teach their fellow classmates but are concerned about quality lessons and may not feel comfortable with the grading aspect of the assignment. Rarely do students understand all of the components that go into designing an effective lesson. This student-taught lesson rubric (see Figure 4.2) helps focus the student on the important aspects of a well-designed lesson and allows teachers to make the evaluation a little more subjective.

Another situation which often needs clarification and focus to assist with time management is oral presentations. There are two rubrics included to assist with this process: one for the evaluation of the speaker by the teacher (see Figure 4.3) and one for feedback from the students (see Figure 4.4). A rubric is included for feedback from the students to encourage active participation on the part of the student observers. This student feedback is always meant to be given in a positive manner. When used with my students, they seemed to value their peers' feedback more than the rubric I gave them with the grades.

Student-Taught Lesson Rubric

Name: _____

Parts of Lesson	Excellent	Good	Fair	Poor	Self
Prepared and Ready All materials and lesson ready at the start of class period, from warm-up to conclusion of lesson.	**10** Everything is ready to present.	**6** Lesson is present, but small amount of scrambling.	**3** Lesson is present, but major scrambling.	**0** No lesson ready or missing major components.	
Understanding Presenter(s) understands the material well. Students understand information presented.	**20** All information is correct and in correct format.	**12** Presenter understands; 25% of students do not.	**4** Presenter understands; 50% of students do not.	**0** Presenter is confused.	
Complete Includes all significant information from section or topic.	**15** Includes all important information.	**10** Includes most important information.	**2** Includes less than 50% of the important information.	**0** Information is not related.	
Practice Includes some way for students to practice the information presented.	**20** Practice present; was well chosen.	**10** Practice present; can be applied effectively.	**5** Practice present; not related or best choice.	**0** No practice or students are confused.	
Interest/Fun Most of the class was involved, interested, and participating.	**15** Everyone interested and participating.	**10** 75% actively participating.	**5** Less than 50% actively participating.	**0** Everyone off task.	
Creativity Information presented in an imaginative way.	**20** Wow, creative! I never would have thought of that!	**12** Good ideas!	**5** Some good pieces but general instruction.	**0** No creativity; all lecture, notes, or worksheet.	

Your Topic/Objective:

Comments:

Don't forget: All copy requests and material requests must be made at least 24 hours in advance.

Figure 4.2. Student-taught lesson rubric.

Oral Presentation Rubric

	Excellent	Good	Fair	Poor	Self
Content—Complete The presentation included everything it should.	**30** Presentation included all of the important information about the topic being presented.	**20** Presentation covered most of the important information, but one key idea was missing.	**10** Presentation covered some of the important information, but more than one key idea was missing.	**0** Presentation included some information, but it was trivial or fluff.	
Content—Correct All of the information presented was accurate.	**30** All of the information presented was accurate.	**20** All of the information presented was correct with a few unintentional errors that were quickly corrected.	**10** Most of the information presented was correct, but there were a few errors.	**0** The information presented was not correct.	
Content—Consistency Speaker stayed on topic during the presentation.	**10** Presenter stayed on topic 100% of the time.	**7** Presenter stayed on topic 90–99% of the time.	**4** Presenter stayed on topic 80–89% of the time.	**0** It was hard to tell what the topic was.	
Prop Speaker had at least one prop that was directly related to the presentation.	**20** Presenter had the prop, and it complemented the presentation.	**12** Presenter had a prop, but it was not the best choice.	**4** Presenter had a prop, but there was no clear reason for its choice.	**0** No prop.	
Flow Speaker knew the presentation well, so the words were well-spoken and flowed well together.	**10** Presentation flowed well. Speaker did not stumble over words.	**7** Some flow problems, but they did not distract from information.	**4** Some flow problems interrupted presentation; presenter seemed flustered.	**0** Constant flow problems; information was not presented in a way it could be understood.	

Total Grade: (100)

Figure 4.3. Oral presentation rubric.

Topic: _____ **Student's Name:** _____

On a scale of 1–10, rate the following areas:

	Your Ranking	
Content (Depth of information. How well did the speaker know his or her information? Was the information correct? Could the speaker answer questions?)	☐	Give one specific reason why you gave this number.
Flow (Did the presentation flow smoothly? Did the speaker appear confident and ready to speak?)	☐	Give one specific reason why you gave this number.
Prop (Did the speaker explain the prop he or she chose? Did the choice seem logical? Was it the best choice?)	☐	Give one specific reason why you gave this number.

Comments: Below, write two specific things that you think the presenter did well.

Topic: _____ **Student's Name:** _____

On a scale of 1–10, rate the following areas:

	Your Ranking	
Content (Depth of information. How well did the speaker know his or her information? Was the information correct? Could the speaker answer questions?)	☐	Give one specific reason why you gave this number.
Flow (Did the presentation flow smoothly? Did the speaker appear confident and ready to speak?)	☐	Give one specific reason why you gave this number.
Prop (Did the speaker explain the prop he or she chose? Did the choice seem logical? Was it the best choice?)	☐	Give one specific reason why you gave this number.

Comments: Below, write two specific things that you think the presenter did well.

Figure 4.4. Student feedback rubric.

PART II

The Menus

How to Use the Menu Pages

Each menu in this section has:
- an introduction page for the teacher that includes the answers to any calculations included on the menu,
- the content menu, and
- any specific activities mentioned in the menu.

Introduction Pages

The introduction pages are meant to provide an overview of each menu. They are divided into five areas.
- *Objectives Covered Through the Menu and Activities.* This area will list all of the instructional objectives that the menu can address. Although all of the objectives integrated into the menus correlate to state and national standards, these targets will be stated in a generic, teacher-friendly way. Menus are arranged in such a way that if students complete the guidelines outlined in the instructions for the menu, all of these objectives will be covered.

- *Materials Needed by Students for Completion.* For each menu, it is expected that the teacher will provide, or students will have access to, the following materials:
  - lined paper,
  - blank 8.5" by 11" white paper,
  - glue, and
  - colored pencils or markers.

  The introduction page also includes a list of additional materials that may be needed by students as they complete the menu. Students do have the choice of the menu items they can complete, so it is possible that the teacher will not need all of these materials for every student.
- *Special Notes on the Use of This Menu.* Some menus allow students to choose to present products to their classmates, build items out of recycled materials, or build quiz boards. This section will outline any special tips on managing products that may require more time, supplies, or space. This section will also share any tips to consider for a particular activity.
- *Time Frame.* Each menu has its ideal time frame based on its structure, but all need at least one week to complete. Menus that assess more objectives are better suited to more than 2 weeks. This section will give you an overview of the best time frame for completing the entire menu, as well as options for shorter time periods. If teachers do not have time to devote to a whole menu, they certainly can choose the 1–2-day option for any menu topic students are currently studying.
- *Suggested Forms.* This section contains a list of the rubrics or forms that should be available for students as the menus are introduced. If a menu has a free-choice option, the appropriate proposal form also will be listed here.

CHAPTER 5

Foundational Skills

20 Points
☐ _____
☐ _____
50 Points
☐ _____
☐ _____
☐ _____
☐ _____
80 Points
☐ _____
☐ _____

Geometric Terms I

20-50-80 Menu

Objectives Covered Through This Menu and These Activities

- Students will distinguish between undefined terms, definitions, and geometric terms.
- Students will create and use representations to organize, record, and communicate mathematical ideas.
- Students will analyze mathematical relationships to connect and communicate mathematical ideas.
- Students will display, explain, and justify mathematical ideas and arguments using precise mathematical language in written or oral communication.

Materials Needed by Students for Completion

- Poster board or large white paper
- Materials for board games (folders, colored cards, etc.)
- Microsoft PowerPoint or other slideshow software
- Magazines (for collages)

Special Notes on the Use of This Menu

- This menu gives students the opportunity to teach a concept. This can take a significant amount of time and organization. It can save time if the students who choose to do a lesson can sign up for a designated day and time that is determined when the menu is distributed.

Time Frame

- 1–2 weeks—Students are given a menu as the unit is started, and the teacher discusses all of the product options on the menu. As the different options are discussed, students will choose the activities they are most interested in completing so that they meet their goal of 100 points. As the lessons progress through the week(s), the teacher and students refer back to the menu options associated with the content being taught.
- 1–2 days—The teacher chooses an activity or product from the menu to use with the entire class.

Suggested Forms

- All-purpose rubric
- Student-taught lesson rubric
- Proposal form for point-based projects
- Presentation rubric

Geometric Terms I

Directions: Choose at least two activities from the menu below. The activities must total 100 points. Place a checkmark next to each box to show which activities you will complete. All activities must be completed by _____ .

As you complete this menu, you must include all of the following geometric terms in your products at least once:

☐ _____   ☐ _____   ☐ _____

☐ _____   ☐ _____   ☐ _____

☐ _____   ☐ _____   ☐ _____

☐ _____   ☐ _____   ☐ _____

☐ _____   ☐ _____   ☐ _____

---

20 Points

☐ Assemble a collage with examples of key geometric terms. Label each picture with the term it represents.

☐ Prepare a "Welcome to Geometry" picture dictionary to help others understand the different terms they will need to use in this class.

---

50 Points

☐ Build a board game to help others practice geometric terms in the world around them.

☐ Assemble a playlist of popular song titles that includes at least four of your geometric terms. Record the list on a poster and include a brief summary of each song as it relates to each term.

☐ Prepare a class game that allows your classmates to practice their knowledge of the geometric terms. Your game should focus not only on the terms themselves, but also on drawings and real-world examples of each.

☐ **Free choice on understanding geometric terms**—Prepare a proposal form and submit it to your teacher for approval.

Geometric Terms I, continued

80 Points

☐ Come to school as Euclid and present a You Be the Person presentation in which you discuss how your findings relate to modern-day geometry.

☐ Record a class lesson in which you teach your classmates about an important geometric theorem. Include examples of and rationale for the theorem you have selected.

Geometric Terms II

One-Topic List Menu

Objectives Covered Through This Menu and These Activities
- Students will distinguish between undefined terms, definitions, and geometric terms.
- Students will communicate mathematical ideas, reasoning, and their implications using multiple representations.
- Students will create and use representations to organize, record, and communicate mathematical ideas.
- Students will analyze mathematical relationships to connect and communicate mathematical ideas.
- Students will display, explain, and justify mathematical ideas and arguments using precise mathematical language in written or oral communication.

Materials Needed by Students for Completion
- Poster board or large white paper
- Coat hangers (for mobiles)
- String (for mobiles)
- Blank index cards (for mobiles, concentration cards)
- Recording software or application (for videos, news reports)
- Graph paper or Internet access (for crossword puzzles)
- Scrapbooking materials
- Large blank lined index cards (for instruction cards)

Special Notes on the Use of This Menu
- This menu gives students the opportunity to create a video and news report. The grading and sharing of these products can often be facilitated by having students prerecord their product using whatever technology is most convenient for the teacher. This allows the teacher to decide when it will be shown as well as keeps the presentation to its intended length. If recording options are limited, this activity can be modified by allowing students to act out the product (like a play) in front of the class.

Time Frame

- 1–2 weeks—Students are given the menu as the unit is started, and the guidelines and point expectations are discussed. Students usually will need to earn 100 points for 100%, although there is an opportunity for extra credit if the teacher would like to use another target number. Because this menu covers one topic in depth, the teacher will go over all of the options for the topic being covered and have students place checkmarks in the boxes next to the activities they are most interested in completing. Teachers will need to set aside a few moments to sign the agreement at the bottom of the page with each student. As instruction continues, activities are completed by students and submitted to the teacher for grading.
- 1–2 days—The teacher chooses an activity or product from an objective to use with the entire class during that lesson time.

Suggested Forms

- All-purpose rubric
- Proposal form for point-based products
- Presentation rubric

Name:_____ Date:_____

Geometric Terms II

Guidelines:

1. You may complete as many of the activities listed as you wish within the time period.
2. You may choose any combination of activities, but **must** complete at least one activity from each topic area.
3. Your goal is 100 points. (This is a grade of 100/100.) You may earn up to _____ points extra credit.
4. You may be as creative as you like within the guidelines listed below.
5. You must show your plan to your teacher by _____ .
6. Activities may be turned in at any time during the working time period. They will be graded and recorded on this sheet as you continue to work, so keep it safe!
7. As you complete this menu, you must include all of the following geometric terms in your products at least once.

☐ _____   ☐ _____   ☐ _____

☐ _____   ☐ _____   ☐ _____

☐ _____   ☐ _____   ☐ _____

☐ _____   ☐ _____   ☐ _____

☐ _____   ☐ _____   ☐ _____

Plan to Do	Activity to Complete	Point Value	Date Completed	Points Earned
	Make a geometric term mobile for at least six of your terms that shares each term, a drawing of each term, and its definition.	10		
	Create a set of three-way set concentration cards (word, drawing, and definition) for at least 10 of your words.	10		
	Write three facts and a fib about two of the geometric terms your classmates might confuse.	15		
	Design an instruction card to distinguish between two similar geometric terms.	15		
	Prepare a mind map to show the relationship between different geometric terms.	15		
	Create a crossword puzzle for the geometric terms. Your clues should include definitions, examples, and drawings.	20		
	Assemble a "Geometry in the Real World" scrapbook in which each page is dedicated to real-world examples of your geometric terms.	20		
	Write and perform an original song that teaches others about the relationships between at least five geometric terms.	25		
	Invent a social media profile for a "family" of geometric terms.	25		
	Perform or record a news report for a recent local event in which the person the reporter interviews about the event only describes the event using geometric terms.	30		
	Record a fun, educational video in which you investigate geometry in the world around us.	30		

Geometric Terms II, continued

	Free Choice: Submit your free-choice proposal form for a product of your choice.			
	Total number of points you are planning to earn.	**Total points earned:**		

I am planning to complete _____ activities that could earn up to a total of _____ points.

Teacher's initials _____ Student's signature _____

CHAPTER 6

Two- and Three-Dimensional Figures

Quadrilaterals

Tic-Tac-Toe Menu

Objectives Covered Through This Menu and These Activities

- Students will prove a quadrilateral is a parallelogram, rectangle, square, or rhombus using opposite sides, opposite angles, or diagonals, and apply these relationships to solve problems.
- Students will communicate mathematical ideas, reasoning, and their implications using multiple representations.
- Students will analyze mathematical relationships to connect and communicate mathematical ideas.

Materials Needed by Students for Completion

- Poster board or large white paper
- Blank index cards (for trading cards, card sorts)
- Recycled materials (for models)
- Graph paper or Internet access (for crossword WebQuests)
- Scrapbooking materials

Special Notes on the Use of This Menu

- This menu asks students to use recycled materials to create their model. This does not mean only plastic and paper; instead, students should focus on using materials in new ways. It works well if a box is started for "recycled" contributions at the beginning of the school year. That way, students always have access to these types of materials.
- This menu allows students to create a WebQuest. There are multiple versions and templates for WebQuests available on the Internet. It is your decision whether you would like to specify a specific format or if you will allow students to create one of their own choosing.

Time Frame

- 2–3 weeks—Students are given the menu as the unit is started. The teacher will go over all of the options for that content and have students place checkmarks in the boxes that represent the activities they are most interested in completing. As students choose activities, they should complete a column or a row. When students complete this pattern, they have completed one activity from each content area, learning style, or level of Bloom's revised taxonomy, depending on the design of the menu. As the teacher presents lessons throughout the week, he or she should refer back to the menu options associated with that content.

- 1 week–At the start of the unit, the teacher chooses the three activities he or she feels are most valuable for students. Stations can be set up in the classroom. These three activities are available for student choice throughout the week as regular instruction takes place.
- 1–2 days—The teacher chooses an activity from the menu to use with the entire class.

Suggested Forms

- All-purpose rubric
- Free-choice proposal form

Name:_____ Date:_____

Quadrilaterals

Directions: Check the boxes you plan to complete. They should form a tic-tac-toe across or down. All products are due by: _____ .

☐ *Properties of Quadrilaterals* Create a set of trading cards for each quadrilateral. Include the relationships between each shape on each card.	☐ *A What Is a What?* Draw a mind map that shows the connectedness between all of the different quadrilaterals.	☐ *Quadrilateral Relationships* Prepare a WebQuest that has questors investigating the relationships between parallelograms, rectangles, squares, and rhombuses.
☐ *Quadrilateral Relationships* Write Three Facts and a Fib about the relationships between parallelograms, rectangles, squares, and rhombuses.	☐ **Free Choice: Properties of Quadrilaterals** (Fill out your proposal form before beginning the free choice!)	☐ *A What Is a What?* Assemble a quadrilateral family scrapbook with a page for each family member. Be sure to include multiple real examples of each family member.
☐ *A What Is a What?* Build a model that could be used to prove that a square is a parallelogram, a rectangle, and a rhombus.	☐ *Quadrilateral Relationships* Design a card sort that could be used to sort real-world quadrilaterals into different groups based on their properties.	☐ *Properties of Quadrilaterals* Make a folded quiz book that tests your classmates' abilities to distinguish the proprieties of different quadrilaterals.

© Prufrock Press Inc. • *Differentiating Instruction With Menus: Geometry* • *Grades 9–12*

Area of a Polygon

20-50-80 Menu

Objectives Covered Through This Menu and These Activities

- Students will apply the formula for the area of regular polygons to solve problems using appropriate units of measure.
- Students will communicate mathematical ideas, reasoning, and their implications using multiple representations.
- Students will display, explain, and justify mathematical ideas and arguments using precise mathematical language in written or oral communication.

Materials Needed by Students for Completion

- Poster board or large white paper
- Microsoft PowerPoint or other slideshow software
- Recording software or application (for videos)
- Large blank lined index cards (for instruction cards)

Special Notes on the Use of This Menu

- This menu gives students the opportunity to create a video. The grading and sharing of these products can often be facilitated by having students prerecord their product using whatever technology is most convenient for the teacher. This allows the teacher to decide when it will be shown as well as keeps the presentation to its intended length. If recording options are limited, this activity can be modified by allowing students to act out the product (like a play) in front of the class.

Time Frame

- 1–2 weeks—Students are given a menu as the unit is started, and the teacher discusses all of the product options on the menu. As the different options are discussed, students will choose the activities they are most interested in completing so that they meet their goal of 100 points. As the lessons progress through the week(s), the teacher and students refer back to the menu options associated with the content being taught.
- 1–2 days—The teacher chooses an activity or product from the menu to use with the entire class.

Suggested Forms
- All-purpose rubric
- Proposal form for point-based projects
- Presentation rubric

Area of a Polygon

Directions: Choose at least two activities from the menu below. The activities must total 100 points. Place a checkmark next to each box to show which activities you will complete. All activities must be completed by _____ .

---

20 Points

☐ Make a folded quiz book for calculating the area of a polygon given different measurements.

☐ Write an instruction card that explains how to find the area of a polygon depending on the measurements provided.

---

50 Points

☐ Make a worksheet that asks students to practice finding apothems, radii, or the number of sides of a polygon when given the area.

☐ Create an area of a polygon Three Facts and a Fib about the Tower of the Winds.

☐ Investigate the use of polygons in the Bomarsund Fortress. Prepare a video in which you discuss the different polygons used and how their areas impacted the structures created.

☐ **Free choice on area of a polygon**—Prepare a proposal form and submit it to your teacher for approval.

---

80 Points

☐ Research the U.S. Pentagon. Prepare a PowerPoint presentation that shows how to calculate the area of the building (not including the grounds in the middle).

☐ On a poster, design an original floor plan for a museum that includes all of the polygons we have discussed. Include a calculation for the total square footage of your museum.

Surface Area

Meal Menu

Objectives Covered Through This Menu and These Activities

- Students will apply the formulas for the total and lateral surface area of three-dimensional figures, including prisms, pyramids, cones, cylinders, spheres, and composite figures, to solve problems using appropriate units of measure.
- Students will apply mathematics to problems found in everyday life.
- Students will use problem-solving models to address real-world problems.
- Students will select appropriate tools to solve problems.
- Students will communicate mathematical ideas, reasoning, and their implications using multiple representations.
- Students will create and use representations to organize, record, and communicate mathematical ideas.
- Students will analyze mathematical relationships to connect and communicate mathematical ideas.

Materials Needed by Students for Completion

- Poster board or large white paper
- Microsoft PowerPoint or other slideshow software
- Method for recording responses to word problems

Special Notes on the Use of This Menu

- This menu is a product and problem menu; it asks students to not only create products to demonstrate their knowledge, but also answer one or more higher level word problems. It is set up in such a way that students will have to complete at least one of the word problems. When introducing this menu, teachers will need to have already determined how they would like these problems completed and recorded for grading. Remember, this is the opportunity to hold high standards when it comes to showing work and defending answers!
- This menu gives students the opportunity to teach a concept. This can take a significant amount of time and organization. It can save time if the students who choose to do a lesson can sign up for a designated day and time that is determined when the menu is distributed.

Time Frame

- 2–3 weeks—Students are given the menu as the unit is started. As the lesson or unit progresses throughout the week, students should refer back to the menu options associated with that content. The teacher will go over all of the options for that objective and have students place a checkmark in the box for each option that represents the activity they are most interested in completing. As teaching continues, the activities chosen and completed should create a full day's meal, with a breakfast, a lunch, a dinner, and an optional dessert. The teacher may choose to allow students time to work after other work is finished. When students complete the menu with this expectation, they have completed one activity from each content area, learning style, or level of Bloom's revised taxonomy, depending on the design of the menu.
- 1 week—At the start of the unit, the teacher chooses one activity from each meal family he or she feels is most valuable for students. Stations can be set up in the classroom. These three activities are available for student choice throughout the week as regular instruction takes place.
- 1–2 days—The teacher chooses an activity or product from an objective to use with the entire class during that lesson time. Additionally, the teacher could choose one of the two desserts as an enrichment activity.

Suggested Forms

- All-purpose rubric
- Student-taught lesson rubric
- Free-choice proposal form

Answers to Menu Problems

Problem 1: A birdhouse has been placed in the school's garden. Your class has been tasked with painting the structure so that others can decorate it. The house itself is square, with sides that are 10 in. long and 8 in. tall. The roof is 5 in. tall. There is a 3 in. diameter hole in the front of the house for the birds to enter. If a half-gallon of paint can cover about 190 ft^2, how much of a half-gallon would you need to paint all of the visible surfaces of the house?

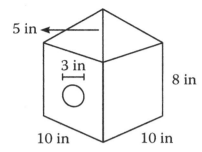
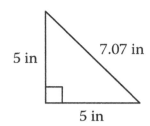

Bottom of house (lateral surface area) = Ph
$$= (40 \text{ in}) (8 \text{ in})$$
$$= 320 \text{ in}^2$$

Hole = πr^2
$$= (3.14) (2.25 \text{ in})$$
$$= 7.065 \text{ in}^2$$

Roof (lateral surface area of pyramid) = $\frac{1}{2}Pl$

$$= \frac{1}{2} (40 \text{ in}) (7.07 \text{ in})$$

$$= 141.4 \text{ in}^2$$

Total area = $320 \text{ in}^2 + 141.4 \text{ in}^2 - 7.065 \text{ in}^2$
$$= 454.3 \text{ in}^2$$
$$= 3.16 \text{ ft}^2$$

$$\frac{1 \text{ half-gallon}}{190 \text{ ft}^2} = \frac{x \text{ half-gallons}}{3.16 \text{ ft}^2}$$

$$x = .017 \text{ half-gallons}$$

Problem 2: Your local transit company has decided to paint its orange traffic cones with reflective paint to make them even more visible. The cones it has chosen have a base diameter of 5 in. and are 18 in. in height, with a square 6 in. wide, 1in. thick base. Assuming the cone is a complete cone and the company wants to paint only visible surfaces, if it has 234 cones in the warehouse and each gallon of reflective paint covers about 250 ft², how much paint would it need?

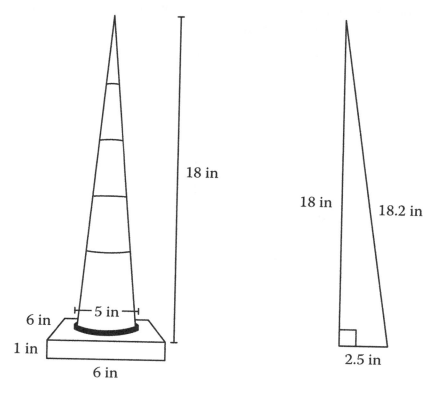

Lateral surface area of cone = $\pi r l$
  = (3.14) (2.5 in) (18.2 in)
  = 142.87 in

Surface of base = lateral surface area + top area − base of cone
  = $Ph + s^2 - \pi r^2$
  = (24 in) (1 in) + (6 in)² − π (2.5 in)²
  = 24 in² + 36 in² − 19.6 in²
  = 40.4 in² per cone

Because there are 234 cones, that means a total of 9,453.6 in² of paint is needed, or 65.65 ft² of paint.

$$\frac{1 \text{ gal}}{250 \text{ ft}^2} = \frac{x \text{ gal}}{65.65 \text{ ft}^2} = .26 \text{ gallons}$$

Problem 3: The Round Barn in Arcadia, OK, is going to be repainted. If the bottom story is 20 ft tall, the diameter is 60 ft, and total height is 45 ft, and one gallon of barn paint will cover about 390 ft², how much paint would it take to coat the barn twice?

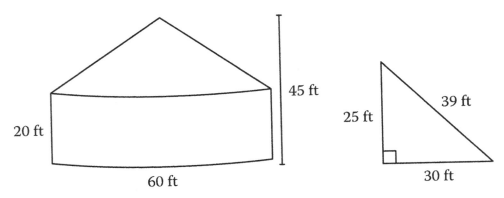

Bottom of the barn (lateral surface area of cylinder) = $2\pi r h$
$$= 2(3.14)\,(30\text{ ft})\,(20\text{ ft})$$
$$= 3{,}768\text{ ft}^2$$

Roof of barn (lateral surface area of cone) = $\pi r l$
$$= (3.14)\,(30\text{ ft})\,(39\text{ ft})$$
$$= 3{,}673.8\text{ ft}^2$$

$$\frac{1\text{ gal}}{390\text{ ft}^2} = \frac{x\text{ gal}}{7{,}441.8\text{ ft}^2} = 19.08\text{ gal}$$

19.08 gal of paint are needed for one coat, or 38.16 gal for two coats.

Surface Area

Directions: Choose one activity each for breakfast, lunch, and dinner. Dessert is an activity you can choose to do after you have finished your other meals. All products must be completed by: _____ .

Breakfast

☐ Assemble a set of concentration cards that allows players to match total and lateral surface area formulas with drawings of each.

☐ Design an original worksheet to help others practice how the total and lateral surface area formulas for different shapes were developed.

☐ Each surface area formula is based on area formulas. Prepare a PowerPoint presentation that shares these relationships for each surface area formula.

Lunch

☐ **Problem 1:** A birdhouse has been placed in the school's garden. Your class has been tasked with painting the structure so that others can decorate it. The house itself is square, with sides that are 10 in. long and 8 in. tall. The roof is 5 in. tall. There is a 3 in. diameter hole in the front of the house for the birds to enter. If a half-gallon of paint can cover about 190 ft^2, how much of a half-gallon would you need to paint all of the visible surfaces of the house?

☐ **Problem 2:** Your local transit company has decided to paint its orange traffic cones with reflective paint to make them even more visible. The cones it has chosen have a base diameter of 5 in. and are 18 in. in height, with a square 6 in. wide, 1 in. thick base. Assuming the cone is a complete cone and the company wants to paint only visible surfaces, if it has 234 cones in the warehouse and each gallon of reflective paint covers about 250 ft^2, how much paint would it need?

☐ **Problem 3:** The Round Barn in Arcadia, OK, is going to be repainted. If the bottom story is 20 ft tall, the diameter is 60 ft, and total height is 45 ft, and one gallon of barn paint will cover about 390 ft^2, how much paint would it take to coat the barn twice?

Dinner

☐ Investigate the measurements of the Stanley Cup. Develop a plan that could be used to determine the amount of silver plate it would take to replate the trophy with a 2 mm thick layer of silver plate. Share your plan on a poster.

☐ A company wants to investigate if larger boxes that hold more product would be more cost efficient than smaller boxes that hold fewer items. If the processing and cutting of the cardboard packaging costs an average of $.0015 per square inch, prepare a video in which you choose a product and analyze which option is most cost efficient for that product.

Surface Area, continued

☐ Research *The Sphere* in New York City. Consider the amount of cleaning product that would be needed to clean this sculpture. If each spray of cleaner uses .3 oz of cleaner, develop a plan to calculate how many bottles of a popular cleaner would be needed to clean this sculpture. You may choose the format to present your plan. Although the sculpture is not a complete sphere, assume it is complete and closed for your plan.

Dessert

☐ **Free choice on surface area**—Prepare a proposal form and submit it to your teacher for approval.

☐ Prepare a class lesson to teach others how to calculate the surface area of various real-world compound shapes.

Composite Area

Tic-Tac-Toe Menu

Objectives Covered Through This Menu and These Activities

- Students will determine the area of composite two-dimensional figures comprised of a combination of triangles, parallelograms, trapezoids, kites, regular polygons, or sectors of circles using appropriate units of measure.
- Students will communicate mathematical ideas, reasoning, and their implications using multiple representations.
- Students will display, explain, and justify mathematical ideas and arguments using precise mathematical language in written or oral communication.

Materials Needed by Students for Completion

- Poster board or large white paper
- Microsoft PowerPoint or other slideshow software
- Recording software or application (for videos)
- Graph paper or Internet access (for WebQuests)

Special Notes on the Use of This Menu

- This menu gives students the opportunity to create a video. The grading and sharing of these products can often be facilitated by having students prerecord their product using whatever technology is most convenient for the teacher. This allows the teacher to decide when it will be shown as well as keeps the presentation to its intended length. If recording options are limited, this activity can be modified by allowing students to act out the product (like a play) in front of the class.
- This menu gives students the opportunity to facilitate a class game. The expectation is that all students in the classroom will play an active role in the game. This may mean that the facilitator may need some additional space and time for his or her game. This can take a significant amount of time and organization. It can save time if all of the students who choose to present their game can sign up for a designated day and time that is determined when the menu is distributed.
- This menu allows students to create a WebQuest. There are multiple versions and templates for WebQuests available on the Internet. It is

your decision whether you would like to specify a specific format or if you will allow students to create one of their own choosing.

Time Frame

- 2–3 weeks—Students are given the menu as the unit is started. The teacher will go over all of the options for that content and have students place checkmarks in the boxes that represent the activities they are most interested in completing. As students choose activities, they should complete a column or a row. When students complete this pattern, they have completed one activity from each content area, learning style, or level of Bloom's revised taxonomy, depending on the design of the menu. As the teacher presents lessons throughout the week, he or she should refer back to the menu options associated with that content.
- 1 week—At the start of the unit, the teacher chooses the three activities he or she feels are most valuable for students. Stations can be set up in the classroom. These three activities are available for student choice throughout the week as regular instruction takes place.
- 1–2 days—The teacher chooses an activity from the menu to use with the entire class.

Suggested Forms

- All-purpose rubric
- Free-choice proposal form
- Presentation rubric

Name:_____ Date:_____

Composite Area

Directions: Check the boxes you plan to complete. They should form a tic-tac-toe across or down. All products are due by: _____ .

You must use each of these figures at least once while completing this menu:

☐ Equilateral triangle   ☐ Rhombus   ☐ Regular polygon

☐ Right triangle   ☐ Trapezoid   ☐ Circle

☐ Parallelogram   ☐ Kite

☐ *Calculating Composite Area* Invent a class game that has your classmates work together to calculate the composite areas of figures one step at a time.	☐ *Creating Composite Figure* Design a composite figure mural that is created from various shapes. Calculate the total area, recording your calculations on the back of your mural.	☐ *Composite Figures Around Us* Locate three objects in your school that, if drawn two-dimensionally, would be composite figures. Make a poster that shows how you would calculate the area of each object.
☐ *Composite Figures Around Us* As a class prank, a group of students have decided they want to wallpaper the Washington Monument. If this were possible, record a video sharing how much wallpaper it would take and how much it would cost.	☐ **Free Choice: Calculating Composite Area** (Fill out your proposal form before beginning the free choice!)	☐ *Creating Composite Figures* Write a children's book in which the main characters are assembling a puzzle of shapes that must fit in a 20 cm by 30 cm frame.
☐ *Creating Composite Figures* Draw a graphic novel in which all of the characters are created from composite shapes. If the larger the total area, the weaker the character, how will your novel end?	☐ *Composite Figures Around Us* To help pay for your new car, you have decided to put an advertising wrap on one side. The company you are advertising will pay you $.75 per square centimeter of the wrap. Develop a PowerPoint Presentation that shares your calculations and how much money you would still owe on your dream car.	☐ *Calculating Composite Area* Prepare a composite area WebQuest in which users visit different websites to help them practice dividing composite figures to calculate the composite area.

```
┌─────────────────┐
│ 20 Points       │
│ □ _____   │
│ □ _____   │
│ 50 Points       │
│ □ _____   │
│ □ _____   │
│ □ _____   │
│ □ _____   │
│ 80 Points       │
│ □ _____   │
│ □ _____   │
└─────────────────┘
```

Changing Dimensions

20-50-80 Menu

Objectives Covered Through This Menu and These Activities

- Students will determine and describe how changes in the linear dimensions of a shape affect its perimeter, area, surface area, or volume.
- Students will apply mathematics to problems found in everyday life.
- Students will communicate mathematical ideas, reasoning, and their implications using multiple representations.
- Students will create and use representations to organize, record, and communicate mathematical ideas.
- Students will analyze mathematical relationships to connect and communicate mathematical ideas.
- Students will display, explain, and justify mathematical ideas and arguments using precise mathematical language in written or oral communication.

Materials Needed by Students for Completion

- Poster board or large white paper
- Blank index cards (for concentration cards)
- Scrapbooking materials
- Recording software or application (for videos)
- Recycled materials (for models)
- Large blank lined index cards (for instruction cards)

Special Notes on the Use of This Menu

- This menu gives students the opportunity to create a video. The grading and sharing of these products can often be facilitated by having students prerecord their product using whatever technology is most convenient for the teacher. This allows the teacher to decide when it will be shown as well as keeps the presentation to its intended length. If recording options are limited, this activity can be modified by allowing students to act out the product (like a play) in front of the class.
- This menu asks students to use recycled materials to create their model. This does not mean only plastic and paper; instead, students should focus on using materials in new ways. It works well if a box

is started for "recycled" contributions at the beginning of the school year. That way, students always have access to these types of materials.

Time Frame

- 1–2 weeks—Students are given a menu as the unit is started, and the teacher discusses all of the product options on the menu. As the different options are discussed, students will choose the activities they are most interested in completing so that they meet their goal of 100 points. As the lessons progress through the week(s), the teacher and students refer back to the menu options associated with the content being taught.
- 1–2 days—The teacher chooses an activity or product from the menu to use with the entire class.

Suggested Forms

- All-purpose rubric
- Proposal form for point-based projects

Changing Dimensions

Directions: Choose at least two activities from the menu below. The activities must total 100 points. Place a checkmark next to each box to show which activities you will complete. All activities must be completed by _____ .

20 Points

☐ Prepare an instruction card to explain how to calculate perimeter, area, surface area, and volume given a change in length.

☐ Make a set of concentration cards in which players match a dimensional change with its impact on perimeter, area, surface area, or volume.

50 Points

☐ Create a model that demonstrates the relationship between linear dimensions and two- and three-dimensional calculations.

☐ Design a worksheet (with an answer key) to help your classmates practice working backward from a new volume to a change in its length or width.

☐ Write a Choose Your Own Adventure story in which readers have to correctly calculate dimensional changes as part of the adventure.

☐ **Free choice on changing dimensions**—Prepare a proposal form and submit it to your teacher for approval.

80 Points

☐ Assemble a scrapbook with real-world applications and benefits of knowing how to change dimensions between different measurements.

☐ Research growing capsules. Record a video in which you discuss how these capsules work and their connection with calculating changing dimensions.

Cross Sections

20-50-80 Menu

20 Points
☐ _____
☐ _____
50 Points
☐ _____
☐ _____
☐ _____
☐ _____
80 Points
☐ _____
☐ _____

Objectives Covered Through This Menu and These Activities
- Students will identify the shapes of two-dimensional cross sections of prisms, pyramids, cylinders, cones, and spheres.
- Students will analyze mathematical relationships to connect and communicate mathematical ideas.
- Students will display, explain, and justify mathematical ideas and arguments using precise mathematical language in written or oral communication.

Materials Needed by Students for Completion
- Poster board or large white paper
- Materials for board games (folders, colored cards, etc.)
- Microsoft PowerPoint or other slideshow software
- Blank index cards (for trading cards, card match)
- Recording software or application (for videos)
- Scrapbooking materials

Special Notes on the Use of This Menu
- This menu gives students the opportunity to create a video. The grading and sharing of these products can often be facilitated by having students prerecord their product using whatever technology is most convenient for the teacher. This allows the teacher to decide when it will be shown as well as keeps the presentation to its intended length. If recording options are limited, this activity can be modified by allowing students to act out the product (like a play) in front of the class.

Time Frame
- 1–2 weeks—Students are given a menu as the unit is started, and the teacher discusses all of the product options on the menu. As the different options are discussed, students will choose the activities they are most interested in completing so that they meet their goal of 100 points. As the lessons progress through the week(s), the teacher and students refer back to the menu options associated with the content being taught.

- 1–2 days—The teacher chooses an activity or product from the menu to use with the entire class.

Suggested Forms

- All-purpose rubric
- Proposal form for point-based projects
- Presentation rubric

Cross Sections

Directions: Choose at least two activities from the menu below. The activities must total 100 points. Place a checkmark next to each box to show which activities you will complete. All activities must be completed by _____ .

20 Points

☐ Make a set of cross section trading cards for all of the two-dimensional shapes created as cross sections of three-dimensional figures.

☐ Assemble a card matching game in which players match cross sections with their corresponding three-dimensional figures.

50 Points

☐ Design a scrapbook of cross sections. Your scrapbook should have at least one page for each two-dimensional shape with photos you have taken of three-dimensional objects that have each cross section.

☐ Prepare a PowerPoint or video quiz that has viewers using cross sections to identify famous three-dimensional landmarks. Stay away from obvious landmarks. Try to stump your audience.

☐ Record a video in which you teach others how to analyze a three-dimensional object to determine its cross section. Your video should include three-dimensional composite figures as examples.

☐ **Free choice on cross sections of three-dimensional figures**—Prepare a proposal form and submit it to your teacher for approval.

80 Points

☐ As a cross section, the circle feels that when you compare it with other cross sections of equal area, the circle always represents the three-dimensional object with the greatest volume. Is this true? Prepare a poster to address the circle's claim.

☐ Write a children's book which uses two-dimensional shapes, three-dimensional shapes, and cross sections as part of the story. The book must be a fictional story (not nonfiction about shapes).

Transformations

Tic-Tac-Toe Menu

Objectives Covered Through This Menu and These Activities

- Students will describe and perform transformations of figures in a plane using coordinate notation.
- Students will identify the sequence of transformations that will carry a given pre-image onto an image on and off the coordinate plane.
- Students will identify and distinguish between reflectional and rotational symmetry in a plane figure.
- Students will communicate mathematical ideas, reasoning, and their implications using multiple representations.
- Students will create and use representations to organize, record, and communicate mathematical ideas.
- Students will display, explain, and justify mathematical ideas and arguments using precise mathematical language in written or oral communication.

Materials Needed by Students for Completion

- Poster board or large white paper
- Blank index cards (for trading cards)
- Recording software or application (for videos)

Special Notes on the Use of This Menu

- This menu gives students the opportunity to create a video. The grading and sharing of these products can often be facilitated by having students prerecord their product using whatever technology is most convenient for the teacher. This allows the teacher to decide when it will be shown as well as keeps the presentation to its intended length. If recording options are limited, this activity can be modified by allowing students to act out the product (like a play) in front of the class.
- This menu gives students the opportunity to facilitate a class model. The expectation is that all students in the classroom will play an active role in the model. This may mean that students need some additional space for their model.
- This menu gives students the opportunity to teach a concept. This can take a significant amount of time and organization. It can save

time if the students who choose to do a lesson can sign up for a designated day and time that is determined when the menu is distributed.

Time Frame

- 2–3 weeks—Students are given the menu as the unit is started. The teacher will go over all of the options for that content and have students place checkmarks in the boxes that represent the activities they are most interested in completing. As students choose activities, they should complete a column or a row. When students complete this pattern, they have completed one activity from each content area, learning style, or level of Bloom's revised taxonomy, depending on the design of the menu. As the teacher presents lessons throughout the week, he or she should refer back to the menu options associated with that content.
- 1 week—At the start of the unit, the teacher chooses the three activities he or she feels are most valuable for students. Stations can be set up in the classroom. These three activities are available for student choice throughout the week as regular instruction takes place.
- 1–2 days—The teacher chooses an activity from the menu to use with the entire class.

Suggested Forms

- All-purpose rubric
- Student-taught lesson rubric
- Free-choice proposal form
- Presentation rubric

Transformations

Directions: Check the boxes you plan to complete. They should form a tic-tac-toe across or down. All products are due by: _____ .

☐ *Transformations* Make a set of trading cards for each transformation we have discussed. Be sure to include at least one real-world example for each.	☐ *Reflections and Rotations* Create your own piece of artwork by using reflections and rotations of a pre-image. Select a product you would like to use to present your artwork.	☐ *Transformation Sequences* Investigate the different patterns in nature that could be replicated through mathematical transformations. Record a video that shares your findings as well as how you could make at least two of these patterns with specific transformation sequences.
☐ *Transformation Sequences* Select one of M. C. Escher's works that contains more than one type of transformation. On a poster, present the original work as well as the transformation sequences used to create his work.	☐ **Free Choice: Transformations** (Fill out your proposal form before beginning the free choice!)	☐ *Reflections and Rotations* Propose a classroom model that demonstrates reflections and rotations on a coordinate plane.
☐ *Reflections and Rotations* One of your classmates commented that reflections and rotations are the same thing depending on how they are written. Develop a student-taught lesson that explains how your classmate could be correct.	☐ *Transformation Sequences* Research the use of tessellation designs in home décor. Prepare a PowerPoint presentation that shares at least two specific designs and the transformation sequences used to create each.	☐ *Transformations* Make a folded flipbook that shows all of the transformations we are studying. Be sure to include an example of each.

Triangle Congruence

Two-Topic List Menu

Objectives Covered Through This Menu and These Activities

- Students will prove two triangles are congruent by applying the side-angle-side, angle-side-angle, side-side-side, angle-angle-side, and hypotenuse-leg congruence conditions.
- Students will apply the definition of congruence to identify congruent figures and their corresponding sides and angles.
- Students will create and use representations to organize, record, and communicate mathematical ideas.
- Students will analyze mathematical relationships to connect and communicate mathematical ideas.
- Students will display, explain, and justify mathematical ideas and arguments using precise mathematical language in written or oral communication.

Materials Needed by Students for Completion

- Poster board or large white paper
- Microsoft PowerPoint or other slideshow software
- Blank index cards (for concentration cards)
- Recording software or application (for videos)
- Scrapbooking materials
- Magazines (for collages)
- Materials for bulletin board display
- Large blank lined index cards (for instruction cards)

Special Notes on the Use of This Menu

- This menu gives students the opportunity to create a video. The grading and sharing of these products can often be facilitated by having students prerecord their product using whatever technology is most convenient for the teacher. This allows the teacher to decide when it will be shown as well as keeps the presentation to its intended length. If recording options are limited, this activity can be modified by allowing students to act out the product (like a play) in front of the class.
- This menu allows students to create a bulletin board display. Some classrooms may only have one bulletin board, so the teacher can

divide the board into sections, or additional classroom wall or hall space can be sectioned off for the creation of these displays. Students can plan their display based on the amount of space they are assigned.

Time Frame

- 1–2 weeks—Students are given the menu as the unit is started, and the guidelines and point expectations are discussed. Students usually will need to earn 100 points for 100%, although there is an opportunity for extra credit if the teacher would like to use another target number. Because this menu covers one topic in depth, the teacher will go over all of the options for the topic being covered and have students place checkmarks in the boxes next to the activities they are most interested in completing. Teachers will need to set aside a few moments to sign the agreement at the bottom of the page with each student. As instruction continues, activities are completed by students and submitted to the teacher for grading.
- 1–2 days—The teacher chooses an activity or product from an objective to use with the entire class during that lesson time.

Suggested Forms

- All-purpose rubric
- Proposal form for point-based products

Name:_____ Date:_____

Triangle Congruence

Guidelines:

1. You may complete as many of the activities listed as you wish within the time period.
2. You may choose any combination of activities, but **must** complete at least one activity from each topic area.
3. Your goal is 75 points. (This is a grade of 75/75.) You may earn up to _____ points extra credit.
4. You may be as creative as you like within the guidelines listed below.
5. You must show your plan to your teacher by _____ .
6. Activities may be turned in at any time during the working time period. They will be graded and recorded on this sheet as you continue to work, so keep it safe!

Topic	Plan to Do	Activity to Complete	Point Value	Date Completed	Points Earned
Congruence Conditions		Make a window pane that shows all of the different congruence conditions with an example of each.	10		
		Write an instruction card that could be used to confirm if two triangles are congruent.	15		
		Create a set of concentration cards in which players match congruent triangles using different congruence conditions. Make them tricky!	20		
		There are some angle-side combinations that do not prove congruency. Make a poster that shows why these combinations do not provide congruency.	25		
		Compose and record an original song to help others remember the difference congruence conditions.	25		
		Record a video teaching your classmates about triangles that may seem congruent but need further investigation to determine their congruency.	30		
A Deeper Look		Assemble a collage of real-world examples of congruent triangles. Label each drawing with its congruence.	15		
		Write Three Facts and a Fib about two noncongruent triangles. Be tricky!	20		
		Choose two triangle congruence statements and prepare a bulletin board display that proves each statement.	20		
		All congruence statements have three components except H-L. Prepare a PowerPoint presentation to show why H-L only needs two components.	25		
		Given two triangles, you could use any (not just the obvious one) congruence condition to prove the two triangles are congruent. Create your own product to prove or disprove this idea.	30		
Any		**Free Choice:** Submit your free-choice proposal form for a product of your choice.			
		Total number of points you are planning to earn.	**Total points earned:**		

I am planning to complete _____ activities that could earn up to a total of _____ points.

Teacher's initials _____ Student's signature _____

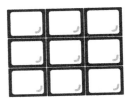

Volume

Game Show Menu

Objectives Covered Through This Menu and These Activities

- Students will apply the formulas for the volume of three-dimensional figures, including prisms, pyramids, cones, cylinders, spheres, and composite figures, to solve problems using appropriate units of measure.
- Students will apply mathematics to problems found in everyday life.
- Students will use problem-solving models to address real-world problems.
- Students will select appropriate tools to solve problems.
- Students will communicate mathematical ideas, reasoning, and their implications using multiple representations.
- Students will create and use representations to organize, record, and communicate mathematical ideas.
- Students will analyze mathematical relationships to connect and communicate mathematical ideas.
- Students will display, explain, and justify mathematical ideas and arguments using precise mathematical language in written or oral communication.

Materials Needed by Students for Completion

- Poster board or large white paper
- Blank index cards (for concentration cards)
- Magazines (for collages)
- Recycled materials (for models)
- Large blank lined index cards (for instruction cards)
- Method for recording responses to word problems

Special Notes on the Use of This Menu

- This menu is a product and problem menu; it asks students to not only create products to demonstrate their knowledge but also answer one or more higher level word problems. It is set up in such a way that students will have to complete at least one of the word problems. When introducing this menu, teachers will need to have already determined how they would like these problems completed and recorded for grading. Remember, this is the opportunity to hold high standards when it comes to showing work and defending answers!

- This menu asks students to use recycled materials to create their model. This does not mean only plastic and paper; instead, students should focus on using materials in new ways. It works well if a box is started for "recycled" contributions at the beginning of the school year. That way, students always have access to these types of materials.

Time Frame

- 2–3 weeks—Students are given their menu as the unit is started and the guidelines and point expectations on the back of the menu are discussed. As lessons are taught throughout the unit, students and the teacher can refer back to the options associated with that topic (or column). The teacher will go over all of the options for the topic being covered and have students place checkmarks in the boxes next to the activities they are most interested in completing. As teaching continues over next 2–3 weeks, activities are discussed, chosen, and submitted for grading.
- 1 week—At the beginning of the unit, the teacher chooses an activity from each area he or she feels would be most valuable for students. Stations can be set up in the classroom or one of the teacher-selected activities could be provided each day for completion. These activities are available for student choice throughout the week as regular instruction takes place.
- 1–2 days—The teacher chooses an activity from an objective to use with the entire class during that lesson time.

Suggested Forms

- All-purpose rubric
- Proposal form for point-based products
- Presentation rubric

Answers to Menu Problems

Problem 1: A large hexagonal aquamarine crystal was just discovered in Brazil. Its sides measure 6 cm and it is 15 cm tall. What is its volume?

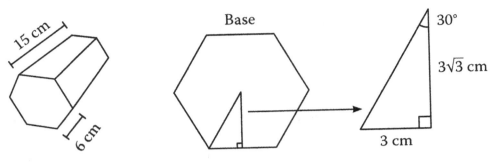

$$\text{Area}_{pologyon} = \frac{1}{2}aP$$

$$= \frac{1}{2}\left(3\sqrt{3} \text{ cm}\right)\left(15 \text{ cm}\right)$$

$$= 54\sqrt{3} \text{ cm}^2 \text{ or } 93.5 \text{ cm}^2$$

$$\text{Volume}_{prism} = Bh$$
$$= (93.5 \text{ cm}^2)(15 \text{ cm})$$
$$= 1{,}402 \text{ cm}^3 \text{ or } 810\sqrt{3} \text{ cm}^3$$

The volume of the crystal is 1,402 cm³.

Problem 2: Research the Pyramid of Cestius and calculate its volume.

The Pyramid of Cestius in Rome has a base of 22 m, with a height of 27 m.

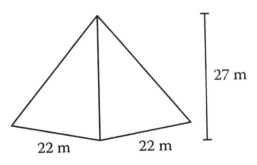

$$\text{Volume}_{\text{pyramid}} = \frac{1}{3}Bh$$

$$= \frac{1}{3}(22 \text{ m})^2(27 \text{ m})$$

$$= \frac{1}{3}(484 \text{ m}^2)(27 \text{ m})$$

$$= 4{,}356 \text{ m}^3$$

The volume of the Pyramid of Cestius is 4,356 m³.

Problem 3: A local charity hung a cone upside down to collect pennies (average .35 cm³). If the cone is 25 cm tall, with a diameter of 15 cm, how much money could it hold assuming no empty space?

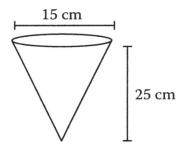

$$\text{Volume}_{\text{cone}} = \frac{1}{3}Bh$$

$$= \frac{1}{3}(\pi r^2)h$$

$$= \frac{1}{3}\pi(7.5 \text{ cm})^2(25 \text{ cm})$$

$$= 468.75\pi \text{ cm}^3 \text{ or } 1{,}472.6 \text{ cm}^3$$

The average penny is .35 cm³, so:

$$\frac{468.75\pi \text{ cm}^3}{.35 \text{ cm}^3} = 1{,}339\pi \text{ pennies}$$

$$\text{or: } \frac{1{,}472.6 \text{ cm}^3}{.35 \text{ cm}^3} = 4{,}207 \text{ pennies}$$

This means that the charity would have approximately $42.07 in the cone if it was filled just to the top.

Problem 4: If a battery contains 95% chemical paste, how much chemical paste is in a standard size C battery?

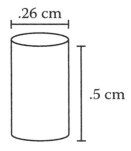

$$
\begin{aligned}
\text{Volume}_{\text{cylinder}} &= Bh \\
&= \pi r^2 h \\
&= \pi \left(.13 \text{ cm}\right)^2 \left(.5 \text{ cm}\right) \\
&= \pi \left(.017 \text{ cm}^2\right)\left(.5 \text{ cm}\right) \\
&= .027 \text{ cm}^3
\end{aligned}
$$

The battery contains 95% chemical paste, so:

$$\left(\frac{95}{100}\right)\left(.027 \text{ cm}^3\right) = .026 \text{ cm}^3$$

The battery contains .026 cm³ or .026 mL of chemical paste.

Problem 5: An IFAF regulation soccer ball must have a circumference between 68 cm and 70 cm. If your school team uses a ball with volume of 6,538 cm³, is your ball regulation?

$$\text{Volume}_{sphere} = \frac{4}{3}\pi r^3$$

$$\frac{3}{4}\left[6{,}538 \text{ cm}^3 = \frac{4}{3}\pi r^3\right]\frac{3}{4}$$

$$\frac{4{,}903.5 \text{ cm}^3}{\pi} = \frac{\pi r^3}{\pi}$$

$$1{,}560.8 \text{ cm}^3 = r^3$$

$$11.6 \text{ cm} = r$$

$$\text{Circumference} = 2\pi r$$
$$= 2\pi\left(11.6 \text{ cm}\right)$$
$$= 72.9 \text{ cm}$$

Because the school's ball has a circumference of 72.9 cm, it is not a regulation ball (as it is currently inflated).

Problem 6: A baker created a three-layer square tiered cake using 2 in. thick layers. The baker made the sides of each layer in a 3:5:7 ratio. If one side of the middle layer measures 10 in., what is the volume of the cake?

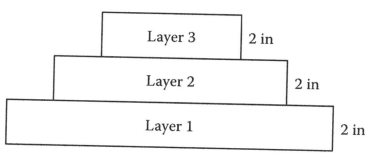

Given the ratio 3:5:7, the cake layers are 6 in:10 in:14 in.

$$\text{Volume}_{prism} = Bh = s^2 h$$

$\text{Volume}_{\text{layer1}} = (14 \text{ in})^2 (2 \text{ in}) = (196 \text{ in}^2)(2 \text{ in}) = 392 \text{ in}^3$

$\text{Volume}_{\text{layer2}} = (10 \text{ in})^2 (2 \text{ in}) = (100 \text{ in}^2)(2 \text{ in}) = 200 \text{ in}^3$

$\text{Volume}_{\text{layer3}} = (6 \text{ in})^2 (2 \text{ in}) = (36 \text{ in}^2)(2 \text{ in}) = 72 \text{ in}^3$

$\text{Total volume} = \text{Volume}_{\text{layer1}} + \text{Volume}_{\text{layer2}} + \text{Volume}_{\text{layer3}}$

$= 392 \text{ in}^3 + 200 \text{ in}^3 + 72 \text{ in}^3$

$= 664 \text{ in}^3$

The total volume of cake is 664 in^3.

Guidelines for the Volume Game Show Menu

- You must choose at least one activity from each topic area.
- You may not do more than two activities in any one topic area for credit. (You are, of course, welcome to do more than two for your own investigation.)
- Grading will be ongoing, so turn in products as you complete them.
- All free-choice proposals must be turned in and approved *prior* to working on the free choice.
- You must earn **200** points for a 100%. You may earn extra credit up to _____ points.
- You must show your teacher your plan for completion by: _____ .

Name:_____ Date:_____

Volume

Prisms	Pyramids	Cones	Cylinders	Spheres	Composite Figures	Points for Each Level
☐ Assemble a collage of real-world prisms. Beside each picture, record how you would calculate its volume using its measurements. (15 pts.)	☐ Design a brochure that explains how to find the area of a pyramid. Include background on how the formula was derived. (10 pts.)	☐ Build a model that shows how the volume of a cone is related to the volume of a cylinder with the same radius and height. (15 pts.)	☐ Make a set of concentration cards in which players match drawings of cylinders (with measurements) with the equations to solve for their volumes. (10 pts.)	☐ Write Three Facts and a Fib about calculating the volume of a real-world sphere. (15 pts.)	☐ Compose an instruction card that details how to calculate the volume of different types of composite figures. Include at least two examples in your explanation. (15 pts.)	**10–15 points**
☐ **Problem 1:** A large hexagonal aquamarine crystal was just discovered in Brazil. Its sides measure 6 cm and it is 15 cm tall. What is its volume? (25 pts.)	☐ **Problem 2:** Research the Pyramid of Cestius and calculate its volume. (20 pts.)	☐ **Problem 3e:** A local charity hung a cone upside down to collect pennies (average .35 cm^3). If the cone is 25 cm tall, with a diameter of 15 cm, how much money could it hold assuming no empty space? (25 pts.)	☐ **Problem 4:** If a battery contains 95% chemical paste, how much chemical paste is in a standard size C battery? (25 pts.)	☐ **Problem 5:** An IFAF regulation soccer ball must have a circumference between 68 cm and 70 cm. If your school team uses a ball with volume of 6,538 cm^3, is your ball regulation? (25 pts.)	☐ **Problem 6:** A baker created a three-layer square tiered cake using 2 in. thick layers. The baker made the sides of each layer in a 3:5:7 ratio. If one side of the middle layer measures 10 in. what is the volume of the cake? (20 pts.)	**20–25 points**
☐ Your teacher made the comment that more than 100,000 ping-pong balls would fit in your gymnasium. Develop a calculation method to see if he or she is right. After taking some measurements, propose the amount that it would hold. (30 pts.)	☐ If the Pyramid of Giza was hollow inside, develop and share a plan to determine how long rescuers would have to save the pharaoh based on his oxygen needs if the pharaoh were accidentally sealed inside once it was completed. (30 pts.)	☐ Mauna Loa, a volcano on Hawai'i is said to have a greater volume than Mauna Kea. Prepare a poster that shows the calculations that support or refute this statement. (30 pts.)	☐ A farmer is deciding on building a custom corn silo for his farm. He grows corn on 60 acres of fields. Based on average yield, what size silo would he need to store all of the grain from his fields. Share your findings in a product of your choice. (30 pts.)	☐ A local basketball team wants to install a large basketball statue outside of their arena. The team wants to be able to say it could hold 100,000 basketballs. Assuming minimum empty space between balls, develop a plan to design the team's statue and share your findings. (30 pts.)	☐ Investigate different brands of classic lunch boxes (have a rectangular bottom and a rounded top). Develop a plan to determine which lunch box provides the most space for the best price. Share your findings in a product of your choice. (30 pts.)	**30 points**
Free Choice (prior approval) (10–30 pts.)	**Free Choice** (prior approval) (10–30 pts.)	**Free Choice** (prior approval) (10–30 pts.)	**Free Choice** (prior approval) (10–30 pts.)	**Free Choice** (prior approval) (10–30 pts.)	**Free Choice** (prior approval) (10–30 pts.)	**10–30 points**
Total:	**Total:**	**Total:**	**Total:**	**Total:**	**Total:**	**Total Grade:**

20 Points
□ _____
□ _____
50 Points
□ _____
□ _____
□ _____
□ _____
80 Points
□ _____
□ _____

Triangles

20-50-80 Menu

Objectives Covered Through This Menu and These Activities
- Students will identify midsegments, altitudes, and medians.
- Students will create and use representations to organize, record, and communicate mathematical ideas.
- Students will analyze mathematical relationships to connect and communicate mathematical ideas.
- Students will display, explain, and justify mathematical ideas and arguments using precise mathematical language in written or oral communication.

Materials Needed by Students for Completion
- Poster board or large white paper
- Microsoft PowerPoint or other slideshow software
- Recording software or application (for videos)
- Recycled materials (for models)

Special Notes on the Use of This Menu
- This menu gives students the opportunity to create two videos. The grading and sharing of these products can often be facilitated by having students prerecord their product using whatever technology is most convenient for the teacher. This allows the teacher to decide when it will be shown as well as keeps the presentation to its intended length. If recording options are limited, this activity can be modified by allowing students to act out the product (like a play) in front of the class.
- This menu asks students to use recycled materials to create their model. This does not mean only plastic and paper; instead, students should focus on using materials in new ways. It works well if a box is started for "recycled" contributions at the beginning of the school year. That way, students always have access to these types of materials.

Time Frame
- 1–2 weeks—Students are given a menu as the unit is started, and the teacher discusses all of the product options on the menu. As the dif-

ferent options are discussed, students will choose the activities they are most interested in completing so that they meet their goal of 100 points. As the lessons progress through the week(s), the teacher and students refer back to the menu options associated with the content being taught.

- 1–2 days—The teacher chooses an activity or product from the menu to use with the entire class.

Suggested Forms

- All-purpose rubric
- Proposal form for point-based projects
- Presentation rubric

Triangles

Directions: Choose at least two activities from the menu below. The activities must total 100 points. Place a checkmark next to each box to show which activities you will complete. All activities must be completed by _____ .

---

20 Points

☐ Write Three Facts and Fib about the relationships between medians and altitudes.

☐ Prepare a children's book that could teach others about altitudes and medians on different types of triangles.

---

50 Points

☐ Record an instructional video that shows how to construct the medians and altitudes of all of the sides of at least four different types of triangles. Be sure your triangles are large enough so that you have room for the constructions!

☐ Build a model that can move to show different types of triangles. Use this model to locate the orthocenter of each type of triangle.

☐ Create a folded quiz book with original drawings and word problems for medians, midsegments, and altitudes that your classmates could solve.

☐ **Free choice on altitudes and medians in triangles**—Prepare a proposal form and submit it to your teacher for approval.

---

80 Points

☐ Investigate the four different centers of a triangle. Record a video that shows how to calculate each of these measurements using a real-world triangle (e.g., pyramid of Giza, glass pyramid by Louvre museum, etc.)

☐ Research the use of triangle shapes in bridge design. Prepare a PowerPoint presentation or bulletin board display to show how the different centers of a triangle impact the effectiveness of the bridge design.

Special Triangles

Tic-Tac-Toe Menu

Objectives Covered Through This Menu and These Activities

- Students will apply the relationships in special right triangles, 30°-60°-90° and 45°-45°-90°, to solve problems.
- Students will apply mathematics to problems found in everyday life.
- Students will use problem-solving models to address real-world problems.
- Students will select appropriate tools to solve problems.
- Students will communicate mathematical ideas, reasoning, and their implications using multiple representations.
- Students will create and use representations to organize, record, and communicate mathematical ideas.
- Students will analyze mathematical relationships to connect and communicate mathematical ideas.
- Students will display, explain, and justify mathematical ideas and arguments using precise mathematical language in written or oral communication.

Materials Needed by Students for Completion

- Poster board or large white paper
- Recording software or application (for videos)
- Graph paper or Internet access (for crossword puzzles, WebQuests)
- Magazines (for collages)
- Method for recording responses to word problems

Special Notes on the Use of This Menu

- This menu is a product and problem menu; it asks students to not only create products to demonstrate their knowledge but also answer one or more higher level word problems. It is set up in such a way that students will have to complete at least one of the word problems. When introducing this menu, teachers will need to have already determined how they would like these problems completed and recorded for grading. Remember, this is the opportunity to hold high standards when it comes to showing work and defending answers!

- This menu gives students the opportunity to create a video. The grading and sharing of these products can often be facilitated by having students prerecord their product using whatever technology is most convenient for the teacher. This allows the teacher to decide when it will be shown as well as keeps the presentation to its intended length. If recording options are limited, this activity can be modified by allowing students to act out the product (like a play) in front of the class.
- This menu gives students the opportunity to teach a concept. This can take a significant amount of time and organization. It can save time if the students who choose to do a lesson can sign up for a designated day and time that is determined when the menu is distributed.

Time Frame

- 2–3 weeks—Students are given the menu as the unit is started. The teacher will go over all of the options for that content and have students place checkmarks in the boxes that represent the activities they are most interested in completing. As students choose activities, they should complete a column or a row. When students complete this pattern, they have completed one activity from each content area, learning style, or level of Bloom's revised taxonomy, depending on the design of the menu. As the teacher presents lessons throughout the week, he or she should refer back to the menu options associated with that content.
- 1 week—At the start of the unit, the teacher chooses the three activities he or she feels are most valuable for students. Stations can be set up in the classroom. These three activities are available for student choice throughout the week as regular instruction takes place.
- 1–2 days—The teacher chooses an activity from the menu to use with the entire class.

Suggested Forms

- All-purpose rubric
- Student-taught lesson rubric
- Free-choice proposal form
- Presentation rubric

Answers to Menu Problems

Problem 1: A child is flying a kite. The kite string is 65 m long. Presently the kite is at a 45° angle with the ground. If the kite moves to a 60° angle with the ground, how much higher is the kite?

Stage 1:

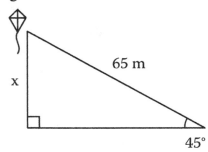

$$\frac{65 \text{ m}}{\sqrt{2}} = \frac{x\sqrt{2}}{\sqrt{2}}$$

$$45.97 \text{ m} = x$$

Stage 2:

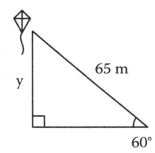

$$\frac{65 \text{ m}}{2} = \frac{2y}{2}$$

$$32.5\sqrt{3} \text{ m} = y$$

Stage 2 − Stage 1 = difference
56.29 m − 45.97 m = 10.32 m

Problem 2: Propose a pair of triangles, a 45-45-90 and a 30-60-90 triangle, that have the same area.

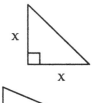

Area of a 45-45-90 triangle = $\frac{1}{2}\left(x^2\right)$

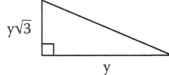

Area of a 30-60-90 triangle = $\frac{1}{2}\left(y^2\sqrt{3}\right)$

By setting the areas equal to each other:

$$2\left[\frac{1}{2}\left(x^2\right) = \frac{1}{2}y^2\sqrt{3}\right]$$

$$\sqrt{x^2 = y^2\sqrt{3}}$$

$$x = \sqrt{y^2\sqrt{3}}$$

Many triangles can be proposed by substituting values for *y* (from the 30-60-90 triangle) and calculating the side (*x*) of the 45-45-90 triangle.

Problem 3: A model builder wants to build an authentic model of an unusual building. He has determined that the outer wall meets the ground at a 60° angle. If the wall is 15 in. tall and 18 in. long, did the builder accomplish his or her goal?

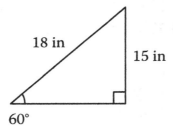
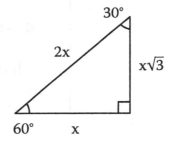

18 in = 2x

9 in = x

If the short side is 9 in., the height will be $9\sqrt{3}$ in., or 15.6 ft, so the builder did not achieve the goal.

Special Triangles

Directions: Check the boxes you plan to complete. They should form a tic-tac-toe across or down. All products are due by: _____ .

☐ *45-45-90 Triangles*	☐ *Problem 1*	☐ *30-60-90 Triangles*
Using a city map (you select the city), create a worksheet that asks questions about calculating distances on the maps using 45-45-90 triangles. Do not forget your answer key!	A child is flying a kite. The kite string is 65 m long. Presently the kite is at a 45° angle with the ground. If the kite moves to a 60° angle with the ground, how much higher is the kite?	Prepare an instructional video that explains how 30-60-90 triangle calculations are used in house building. Include as well at least one specific example with calculations.
☐ *30-60-90 Triangles*	☐ **Free Choice: 45-45-90 Triangle** (Fill out your proposal form before beginning the free choice!)	☐ *Problem 2*
Assemble a collage of real-world objects that contain 30-60-90 triangles. Measure the shortest of each triangle and calculate the other sides. Record your calculations on the collage next to each picture.		Propose a pair of triangles, a 45-45-90 and a 30-60-90 triangle, that have the same area.
☐ *Problem 3*	☐ *30-60-90 Triangles*	☐ *45-45-90 Triangles*
A model builder wants to build an authentic model of an unusual building. He has determined that the outer wall meets the ground at a 60° angle. If the wall is 15 in. tall and 18 in. long, did the builder accomplish his or her goal?	Record a student-taught lesson that teaches others about the ratios between the sides of a 30-60-90 triangle as well as how we can calculate all of the sides, given one.	Design a "mathword" (crossword) puzzle in which players complete the puzzle by solving various real-world 45-45-90 triangle word problem clues.

20 Points
☐ _____
☐ _____
50 Points
☐ _____
☐ _____
☐ _____
☐ _____
80 Points
☐ _____
☐ _____

Pythagorean Theorem

20-50-80 Menu

Objectives Covered Through This Menu and These Activities

- Students will understand and solve problems using the Pythagorean theorem.
- Students will apply mathematics to problems found in everyday life.
- Students will use problem-solving models to address real-world problems.
- Students will communicate mathematical ideas, reasoning, and their implications using multiple representations.
- Students will analyze mathematical relationships to connect and communicate mathematical ideas.
- Students will display, explain, and justify mathematical ideas and arguments using precise mathematical language in written or oral communication.

Materials Needed by Students for Completion

- Poster board or large white paper
- Microsoft PowerPoint or other slideshow software
- Blank index cards (for mobiles, trading cards, card sorts, concentration cards)
- Internet access (Google Maps)
- Large blank lined index cards (for instruction cards)
- Recording software or application (for videos)
- Scrapbooking materials
- Magazines (for collages)

Special Notes on the Use of This Menu

- This menu gives students the opportunity to create a video. The grading and sharing of these products can often be facilitated by having students prerecord their product using whatever technology is most convenient for the teacher. This allows the teacher to decide when it will be shown as well as keeps the presentation to its intended length. If recording options are limited, this activity can be modified by allowing students to act out the product (like a play) in front of the class.

Time Frame

- 1–2 weeks—Students are given a menu as the unit is started, and the teacher discusses all of the product options on the menu. As the different options are discussed, students will choose the activities they are most interested in completing so that they meet their goal of 100 points. As the lessons progress through the week(s), the teacher and students refer back to the menu options associated with the content being taught.
- 1–2 days—The teacher chooses an activity or product from the menu to use with the entire class.

Suggested Forms

- All-purpose rubric
- Student-taught lesson rubric
- Proposal form for point-based projects
- Presentation rubric

Name:_____ Date:_____

Pythagorean Theorem

Directions: Choose at least two activities from the menu below. The activities must total 100 points. Place a checkmark next to each box to show which activities you will complete. All activities must be completed by _____ .

---

20 Points

- ❑ Research how computer monitors are sized. Create a poster that identifies three to four different models and evaluates the accuracy of their published measurements.

- ❑ Assemble a real-world right triangle scrapbook. On each page, record the measurements of two of the sides of the triangular items in each photo and calculate the missing side using your measurements.

---

50 Points

- ❑ Using Google Maps, write an instruction card that could be used to determine if the Flatiron Building in New York City is a right triangle. Include your calculations as an example on the card.

- ❑ You have decided to climb the Diamond Head Summit Trail. Write a newspaper article that shares your research about the trail and calculations for the horizontal distance of your hike to the nearest meter.

- ❑ A climber is interested in climbing the face of The Great Pyramid of Giza. Prepare a PowerPoint presentation that shares information about the pyramid and how you can calculate the length of the face from the ground to the top.

- ❑ **Free choice on real-world Pythagorean examples**—Prepare a proposal form and submit it to your teacher for approval.

---

80 Points

- ❑ Research different examples of the Pythagorean theorem in the world around us. Record an informational video in which you explore these examples. This menu includes real-world examples; your video should share original examples.

- ❑ Prepare a social media profile for the Pythagorean theorem. Consider what other inanimate objects might want to be friends as well as the types of unique interactions they might have. Be creative!

Trigonometry

Three-Topic List Menu

Objectives Covered Through This Menu and These Activities

- Students will determine the lengths of sides and measures of angles in a right triangle by applying the trigonometric ratios sine, cosine, and tangent to solve problems.
- Students will apply mathematics to problems found in everyday life.
- Students will use problem-solving models to address real-world problems.
- Students will create and use representations to organize, record, and communicate mathematical ideas.
- Students will analyze mathematical relationships to connect and communicate mathematical ideas.
- Students will display, explain, and justify mathematical ideas and arguments using precise mathematical language in written or oral communication.

Materials Needed by Students for Completion

- Poster board or large white paper
- Microsoft PowerPoint or other slideshow software
- Materials for three-dimensional timelines
- Recording software or application (for videos, class lesson)
- Scrapbooking materials
- Magazines (for collages)
- Materials for bulletin board display
- Large blank lined index cards (for instruction cards)
- Method for recording responses to word problems

Special Notes on the Use of This Menu

- This menu is a product and problem menu; it asks students to not only create products to demonstrate their knowledge but also answer one or more higher level word problems. It is set up in such a way that students will have to complete at least one of the word problems. When introducing this menu, teachers will need to have already determined how they would like these problems completed and recorded for grading. Remember, this is the opportunity to hold high standards when it comes to showing work and defending answers!

- This menu gives students the opportunity to record a video and class lesson. The grading and sharing of these products can often be facilitated by having students prerecord their product using whatever technology is most convenient for the teacher. This allows the teacher to decide when it will be shown as well as keeps the presentation to its intended length. If recording options are limited, this activity can be modified by allowing students to act out the product (like a play) in front of the class.

- This menu allows students to create a bulletin board display. Some classrooms may only have one bulletin board, so the teacher can divide the board into sections, or additional classroom wall or hall space can be sectioned off for the creation of these displays. Students can plan their display based on the amount of space they are assigned.

Time Frame

- 1–2 weeks—Students are given the menu as the unit is started, and the guidelines and point expectations are discussed. Students usually will need to earn 100 points for 100%, although there is an opportunity for extra credit if the teacher would like to use another target number. Because this menu covers one topic in depth, the teacher will go over all of the options for the topic being covered and have students place checkmarks in the boxes next to the activities they are most interested in completing. Teachers will need to set aside a few moments to sign the agreement at the bottom of the page with each student. As instruction continues, activities are completed by students and submitted to the teacher for grading.

- 1–2 days—The teacher chooses an activity or product from an objective to use with the entire class during that lesson time.

Suggested Forms

- All-purpose rubric
- Student-taught lesson rubric
- Proposal form for point-based products
- Presentation rubric

Answers to Menu Problems

Problem 1: A fire breaks out in a building 30 m above the ground. If the firetruck has a ladder that is 41 m long and can be safely raised from the ground at angle of 70°, will the ladder be able to take the responders up to the fire?

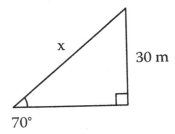

$$\sin 70° = \frac{30 \text{ m}}{\text{x}}$$

$$\text{x} = \frac{30 \text{ m}}{\sin 70°}$$

$$\text{x} = 31.93 \text{ m}$$

The ladder will reach the fire.

Problem 2: Coe Sekant decided to build a water balloon ramp that could transport water balloons from his bedroom window to unsuspecting pedestrians below. His window is 6 m above the ground and his ramp is currently 5 m long. He would like the balloons to drop from at least 3 m in the air. What angle of depression would he need to use to accomplish his goal? How far from the building would his balloons fall?

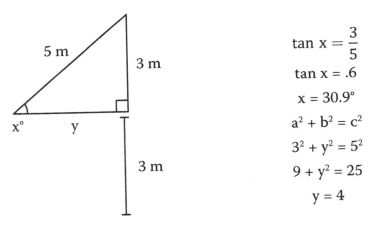

$$\tan \text{x} = \frac{3}{5}$$

$$\tan \text{x} = .6$$

$$\text{x} = 30.9°$$

$$a^2 + b^2 = c^2$$

$$3^2 + y^2 = 5^2$$

$$9 + y^2 = 25$$

$$y = 4$$

He would need to use a 31° angle of depression. The balloon would fall 4 ft from the building.

Problem 3: An airplane at an altitude of 20,000 ft about the ocean sees two boats. The pilot observes the first boat at a 53° angle of depression, the other at a 19° angle of depression. How many miles far apart are the boats?

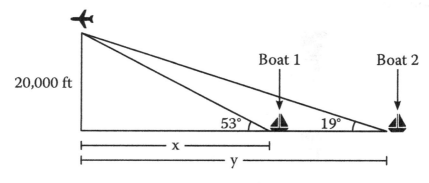

$$\tan 53° = \frac{20,000}{x}$$

$$\frac{x \tan 53°}{\tan 53°} = \frac{20,000}{\tan 53°}$$

$$x = 15,071.01 \text{ ft}$$

$$\tan 19° = \frac{20,000}{y}$$

$$\frac{y \tan 19°}{\tan 19°} = \frac{20,000}{\tan 19°}$$

$$y = 58,084.22 \text{ ft}$$

They are 43,013.21 ft apart or 8.15 mi apart.

Problem 4: Tani Gent is riding up in a hot air balloon that is tethered to the ground. Tani spots a parked car on the ground at an angle of depression of 25°. The balloon rises 100 more meters. Now the angle of depression to the car is 43°. If there is no wind, how far is the car from where the balloon is tethered?

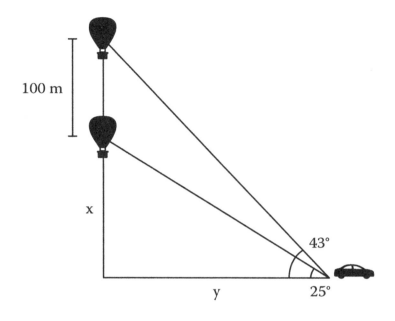

$$\tan 25° = \frac{x}{y}$$

$$y = \tan 25°$$

$$\tan 43° = \frac{x+100}{y}$$

$$y = \frac{x+100}{\tan 43°}$$

$$\frac{x}{\tan 25°} = \frac{x+100}{\tan 43°}$$

$$\tan 43°x = \tan 25° \,(x +100)$$

$$.9325x = .4663x + 46.63$$

$$.4662\,x = 46.63$$

$$x = 100$$

$$\tan 25^\circ = \frac{100}{y}$$

$$y = \frac{100}{\tan 25^\circ}$$

The distance is 214.5 m.

Name:_____ Date:_____

Trigonometry

Guidelines:

1. You may complete as many of the activities listed as you wish within the time period.
2. You may choose any combination of activities, but **must** complete at least one activity from each topic area.
3. Your goal is 100 points. (This is a grade of 100/100.) You may earn up to _____ points extra credit.
4. You may be as creative as you like within the guidelines listed below.
5. You must show your plan to your teacher by _____ .
6. Activities may be turned in at any time during the working time period. They will be graded and recorded on this sheet as you continue to work, so keep it safe!

Topic	Plan to Do	Activity to Complete	Point Value	Date Completed	Points Earned
Equations		Make a poster that shows the sine, cosine, and tangent on a right triangle.	10		
		Create an acrostic for the word *trigonometry*. Your clues must include how to calculate sine, cosine, and tangent.	15		
		Design an original bulletin board display that shares how to use trigonometric relationships to solves for the sides and angles in a right triangle.	15		
		Research how sine and cosine can be used to determines sides and angles of triangles that are not right triangles. Record a student-taught lesson that shows your findings.	25		
Using Trigonometric Equations		Compose an instruction card that explains how to calculate all of the angles in a right triangle given two side measures. Include an example to illustrate the steps.	15		
		Write Three Facts and a Fib about how to set up sine, cosine, and tangent problems given sides of a right triangles.	20		
		The Washington Monument is said to be 555 ft tall. Record a video in which you discuss one way that you could confirm that height through in-person calculations without having to climb the monument itself.	25		
		We did not always have calculators to solve trigonometric problems. Research how students solved for the sides and angles of a right triangle without using a calculator. Prepare a PowerPoint presentation to share your findings.	30		

Trigonometry, continued

Topic	Plan to Do	Activity to Complete	Point Value	Date Completed	Points Earned
Trigonometric Word Problems		**Problem 1:** A fire breaks out in a building 30 m above the ground. If the firetruck has a ladder that is 41 m long and can be safely raised from the ground at angle of 70°, will the ladder be able to take the responders up to the fire?	15		
		Problem 2: Coe Sekant decided to build a water balloon ramp that could transport water balloons from his bedroom window to unsuspecting pedestrians below. His window is 6 m above the ground and his ramp is currently 5 m long. He would like the balloons to drop from at least 3 m in the air. What angle of depression would he need to use to accomplish his goal? How far from the building would his balloons fall?	20		
		Problem 3: An airplane at an altitude of 20,000 ft about the ocean sees two boats. The pilot observes the first boat at a 53° angle of depression, the other at a 19° angle of depression. How many miles far apart are the boats?	25		
		Problem 4: Tani Gent is riding up in a hot air balloon that is tethered to the ground. Tani spots a parked car on the ground at an angle of depression of 25°. The balloon rises 100 more meters. Now the angle of depression to the car is 43°. If there is no wind, how far is the car from where the balloon is tethered?	30		
Any		**Free Choice:** Submit your free-choice proposal form for a product of your choice.			
		Total number of points you are planning to earn.	**Total points earned:**		

I am planning to complete _____ activities that could earn up to a total of _____ points.

Teacher's initials _____ Student's signature _____

CHAPTER 7

Lines

Distance and Midpoint

Tic-Tac-Toe Menu

Objectives Covered Through This Menu and These Activities

- Students will use the distance and midpoint formulas to verify geometric relationships.
- Students will prove equidistance between the endpoints of a segment and points on its perpendicular bisector and apply these relationships to solve problems.
- Students will apply mathematics to problems found in everyday life.
- Students will use problem-solving models to address real-world problems.
- Students will analyze mathematical relationships to connect and communicate mathematical ideas.
- Students will display, explain, and justify mathematical ideas and arguments using precise mathematical language in written or oral communication.

Materials Needed by Students for Completion

- Poster board or large white paper
- Microsoft PowerPoint or other slideshow software
- Blank index cards (for card sorts)
- Graph paper or Internet access (for crossword puzzles)
- Materials for bulletin board display
- Method for recording responses to word problems

Special Notes on the Use of This Menu

- This menu is a product and problem menu; it asks students to not only create products to demonstrate their knowledge but also answer one or more higher-level word problems. It is set up in such a way that students will have to complete at least one of the word problems. When introducing this menu, teachers will need to have already determined how they would like these problems completed and recorded for grading. Remember. this is the opportunity to hold high standards when it comes to showing work and defending answers!
- This menu allows students to create a bulletin board display. Some classrooms may only have one bulletin board, so the teacher can

divide the board into sections, or additional classroom wall or hall space can be sectioned off for the creation of these displays. Students can plan their display based on the amount of space they are assigned.

Time Frame

- 2–3 weeks—Students are given the menu as the unit is started. The teacher will go over all of the options for that content and have students place checkmarks in the boxes that represent the activities they are most interested in completing. As students choose activities, they should complete a column or a row. When students complete this pattern, they have completed one activity from each content area, learning style, or level of Bloom's revised taxonomy, depending on the design of the menu. As the teacher presents lessons throughout the week, he or she should refer back to the menu options associated with that content.
- 1 week—At the start of the unit, the teacher chooses the three activities he or she feels are most valuable for students. Stations can be set up in the classroom. These three activities are available for student choice throughout the week as regular instruction takes place.
- 1–2 days—The teacher chooses an activity from the menu to use with the entire class.

Suggested Forms

- All-purpose rubric
- Free-choice proposal form
- Presentation rubric

Answers to Menu Problems

Problem 1: Wildlife experts tracked a tagged animal after its release. It went $\frac{1}{4}$ of a mile north before going 1 mi east, $\frac{1}{2}$ mi south, and 2 mi east. How far is it from the release point now?

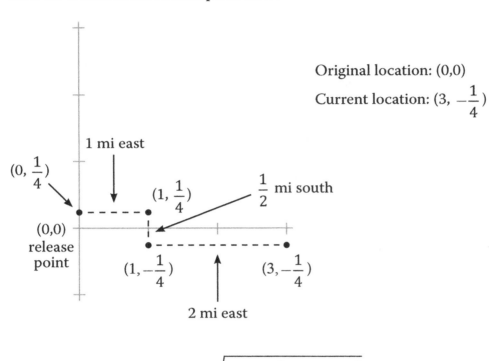

Original location: (0,0)

Current location: $(3, -\frac{1}{4})$

$$\text{distance} = \sqrt{\left(x_2-x_1\right)^2+\left(y_2-y_1\right)^2}$$

$$= \sqrt{\left(0-3\right)^2+\left(0-\left(-\frac{1}{4}\right)\right)^2}$$

$$= \sqrt{\left(-3\right)^2+\left(\frac{1}{4}\right)^2}$$

$$= \sqrt{9+\frac{1}{16}}$$

$$= \sqrt{9.0625} \text{ mi}$$

$$= 3.01 \text{ mi}$$

Problem 2: A bicyclist traveled a total distance of 103 mi on two roads that run perpendicular to each other. If his or her trip ended 89 mi (as the crow flies) from the starting point, what is one possible combination of distances he or she biked on each road?

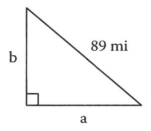

$a^2 + b^2 = 7{,}921$ mi

$a + b = 103$ mi

$a = 103 - b$

$a^2 + b^2 = 7{,}921$ mi

$(103 - b)^2 + b^2 = 7{,}921$ mi

$10{,}609 - 206b + b^2 + b^2 = 7{,}921$ mi

$$\frac{2{,}688 - 206b + 2b^2 = 0}{2}$$

$$b^2 - 103b + 1{,}344 = 0$$

$$\frac{103 \pm \sqrt{(103)^2 - 4(1)(1{,}344)}}{2}$$

$$\frac{103 \pm \sqrt{10{,}609 - 5{,}376}}{2}$$

$$\frac{103 \pm \sqrt{5233}}{2} = \frac{103 + 72.3}{2} \text{ or } \frac{103 - 72.3}{2} = 87.65 \text{ mi or } 15.35 \text{ mi}$$

One option is 87.65 mi on one road and 15.35 mi on the other road.

Problem 3: You want to install a zip line from a tower that is 40 m tall. If you want to it to end a meter and a half off the ground, 100 m from the tower, how long will the zip line be?

$$\text{distance} = \sqrt{\left(x_2 - x_1\right)^2 + \left(y_2 - y_1\right)^2}$$

$$d = \sqrt{\left(-100 - 0\right)^2 + \left(1.5 - 40\right)^2}$$

$$d = \sqrt{\left(100\right)^2 + \left(-38.5\right)^2}$$

$$d = \sqrt{10{,}000 + 1{,}482.25}$$

$$d = \sqrt{11{,}482.25}$$

$$d = 107.15 \text{ m}$$

Name:_____ Date:_____

Distance and Midpoint

Directions: Check the boxes you plan to complete. They should form a tic-tac-toe across or down. All products are due by: _____ .

☐ *Midpoint Formula*	☐ *Problem 1*	☐ *Distance Formula*
Prepare a poster to explain the reasoning (calculations) behind the midpoint formula.	Wildlife experts tracked a tagged animal after its release. It went $\frac{1}{4}$ of a mile north before going 1 mi east, $\frac{1}{2}$ mi south, and 2 mi east. How far is it from the release point now?	Develop a PowerPoint presentation to show the relationship between the Pythagorean theorem and the distance formula.
☐ *Distance Formula*	☐ **Free Choice: Midpoint Formula** (Fill out your proposal form before beginning the free choice!)	☐ *Problem 2*
Design a numerical crossword puzzle (where the answers are numbers). Use distance problems as your clues.		A bicyclist traveled a total distance of 103 mi on two roads that run perpendicular to each other. If his or her trip ended 89 mi (as the crow flies) from the starting point, what is one possible combination of distances he or she biked on each road?
☐ *Problem 3*	☐ *Distance Formula*	☐ *Midpoint Formula*
You want to install a zip line from a tower that is 40 m tall. If you want to it to end a meter and a half off the ground, 100 m from the tower, how long will the zip line be?	Place a coordinate grid over a local map. Use the grid to calculate the distance between two points in your community. Compare your calculations with the map. Share your process on a bulletin board display.	Create a card sort to separate correct and incorrect uses of the midpoint formula to solve real-world problems.

Parallel Lines

Meal Menu

Objectives Covered Through This Menu and These Activities

- Students will verify theorems about angles formed by the intersection of lines and line segments, including vertical angles, and angles formed by parallel lines cut by a transversal.
- Students will use problem-solving models to address real-world problems.
- Students will create and use representations to organize, record, and communicate mathematical ideas.
- Students will display, explain, and justify mathematical ideas and arguments using precise mathematical language in written or oral communication.

Materials Needed by Students for Completion

- Poster board or large white paper
- Materials for board games (folders, colored cards, etc.)
- Blank index cards (for trading cards)
- Recording software or application (for videos)
- Graph paper or Internet access (for WebQuests)
- Recycled materials (for museum exhibits)

Special Notes on the Use of This Menu

- This menu gives students the opportunity to create a video. The grading and sharing of these products can often be facilitated by having students prerecord their product using whatever technology is most convenient for the teacher. This allows the teacher to decide when it will be shown as well as keeps the presentation to its intended length. If recording options are limited, this activity can be modified by allowing students to act out the product (like a play) in front of the class.
- This menu asks students to use recycled materials to create their museum exhibit. This does not mean only plastic and paper; instead, students should focus on using materials in new ways. It works well if a box is started for "recycled" contributions at the beginning of the school year. That way, students always have access to these types of materials.

- This menu gives students the opportunity to facilitate a class model. The expectation is that all students in the classroom will play an active role in the model. This may mean that students need some additional space for their model.
- This menu allows students to create a WebQuest. There are multiple versions and templates for WebQuests available on the Internet. It is your decision whether you would like to specify a specific format or if you will allow students to create one of their own choosing.

Time Frame

- 2–3 weeks—Students are given the menu as the unit is started. As the lesson or unit progresses throughout the week, students should refer back to the menu options associated with that content. The teacher will go over all of the options for that objective and have students place a checkmark in the box for each option that represents the activity they are most interested in completing. As teaching continues, the activities chosen and completed should create a full day's meal, with a breakfast, a lunch, a dinner, and an optional dessert. The teacher may choose to allow students time to work after other work is finished. When students complete the menu with this expectation, they have completed one activity from each content area, learning style, or level of Bloom's revised taxonomy, depending on the design of the menu.
- 1 week—At the start of the unit, the teacher chooses one activity from each meal family he or she feels is most valuable for students. Stations can be set up in the classroom. These three activities are available for student choice throughout the week as regular instruction takes place.
- 1–2 days—The teacher chooses an activity or product from an objective to use with the entire class during that lesson time. Additionally, the teacher could choose one of the two desserts as an enrichment activity.

Suggested Forms

- All-purpose rubric
- Free-choice proposal form
- Presentation rubric

Name:_____ Date:_____

Parallel Lines

Directions: Choose one activity each for breakfast, lunch, and dinner. Dessert is an activity you can choose to do after you have finished your other meals. All products must be completed by: _____ .

Breakfast

❏ Make a set of trading cards for each theorem that addresses the relationships between the angles created by transversal and parallel lines.

❏ Invent a class model that demonstrates the relationships between the angles created by a traversal and parallel lines.

❏ Write and perform an original children's song (with hand motions) that could teach children about the angle relationships between parallel lines and transversals.

Lunch

❏ Consult a local or state road map and find a real-world example of parallel lines and a transversal. On a poster, provide the map and describe the area you located by using its angles.

❏ Consider how these concepts are used in art. Prepare a WebQuest that allows questors to experience parallel lines and angles through an artistic lens.

❏ **Free choice on real-world parallel lines and transversals**—Prepare a proposal form and submit it to your teacher for approval.

Dinner

❏ Write a choose-your-own-adventure story in which readers follow a path of vertical, corresponding, and alternate exterior experiences as part of the plot.

❏ Create a board game in which players investigate parallel lines by moving through parallel lines and their angles created by multiple transversals.

❏ Design a social media profile for the corresponding angles created by a transversal and parallel lines. Consider their interactions with other nearby angles and their connections.

Dessert

❏ Investigate how parallel lines and transversal angles are used in manufacturing specific products. Prepare a video that shares your findings.

❏ Build a museum exhibit that could teach visitors about parallel lines in the world around them.

20 Points
- ☐ _____
- ☐ _____

50 Points
- ☐ _____
- ☐ _____
- ☐ _____
- ☐ _____

80 Points
- ☐ _____
- ☐ _____

Parallel and Perpendicular Lines

20-50-80 Menu

Objectives Covered Through This Menu and These Activities
- Students will determine the slope of parallel and perpendicular lines.
- Students will use slope to predict the equations of parallel and perpendicular lines.
- Students will communicate mathematical ideas, reasoning, and their implications using multiple representations.
- Students will create and use representations to organize, record, and communicate mathematical ideas.
- Students will analyze mathematical relationships to connect and communicate mathematical ideas.
- Students will display, explain, and justify mathematical ideas and arguments using precise mathematical language in written or oral communication.

Materials Needed by Students for Completion
- Poster board or large white paper
- Materials for board games (folders, colored cards, etc.)
- Recording software or application (for videos)
- Scrapbooking materials
- Recycled materials (for models)

Special Notes on the Use of This Menu
- This menu gives students the opportunity to create a video. The grading and sharing of these products can often be facilitated by having students prerecord their product using whatever technology is most convenient for the teacher. This allows the teacher to decide when it will be shown as well as keeps the presentation to its intended length. If recording options are limited, this activity can be modified by allowing students to act out the product (like a play) in front of the class.
- This menu asks students to use recycled materials to create their model. This does not mean only plastic and paper; instead, students should focus on using materials in new ways. It works well if a box is started for "recycled" contributions at the beginning of the school year. That way, students always have access to these types of materials.

- This menu gives students the opportunity to demonstrate a concept. This can take a significant amount of time and organization. It can save time if the demonstration is prerecorded (using whatever technology is most convenient) to share at a later time. If the teacher prefers "live" demonstrations, all of the students who choose to do a demonstration can sign up for a designated day and time that is determined when the menu is distributed.

Time Frame

- 1–2 weeks—Students are given a menu as the unit is started, and the teacher discusses all of the product options on the menu. As the different options are discussed, students will choose the activities they are most interested in completing so that they meet their goal of 100 points. As the lessons progress through the week(s), the teacher and students refer back to the menu options associated with the content being taught.
- 1–2 days—The teacher chooses an activity or product from the menu to use with the entire class.

Suggested Forms

- All-purpose rubric
- Proposal form for point-based projects
- Presentation rubric

Parallel and Perpendicular Lines

Directions: Choose at least two activities from the menu below. The activities must total 100 points. Place a checkmark next to each box to show which activities you will complete. All activities must be completed by _____ .

---

20 Points

❑ Write Three Facts and a Fib about the slopes of parallel and perpendicular lines.

❑ Design a quiz book of tricky parallel and perpendicular lines plotted on coordinate planes.

---

50 Points

❑ Write a story about a line with the equation $2x - 4y = 10$ who is looking for a parallel or perpendicular mate.

❑ Assemble a board game that has players predicting parallel and perpendicular line equations and predicting parallel and perpendicular equations given a point.

❑ Create a model that could be used to demonstrate the mathematics behind parallel and perpendicular slopes. Use different equations to demonstrate your model.

❑ **Free choice on slopes of parallel and perpendicular lines**—Prepare a proposal form and submit it to your teacher for approval.

---

80 Points

❑ Create a parallel and perpendicular scrapbook. Your scrapbook should be filled with photos you have taken in the community that you think represent parallel and perpendicular structures. Put each photo onto a coordinate plane, determine equations for each structure, and provide a statement to express whether each is parallel or perpendicular.

❑ Using a city map, prepare a route between two places that would require traveling on roads that are parallel and perpendicular to each other. Record a video in which you give directions from one place to the other using the equations of the lines created by the roads on the map.

CHAPTER 8

Circles

Circles

20-50-80 Menu

Objectives Covered Through This Menu and These Activities

- Students will show that the equation of a circle with center at the origin and radius r is $x^2 + y^2 = r^2$ and determine the equation for the graph of a circle with radius r and center (h, k), $(x - h)^2 + (y - k)^2 = r^2$.
- Students will create and use representations to organize, record, and communicate mathematical ideas.
- Students will analyze mathematical relationships to connect and communicate mathematical ideas.
- Students will display, explain, and justify mathematical ideas and arguments using precise mathematical language in written or oral communication.

Materials Needed by Students for Completion

- Poster board or large white paper
- Recording software or application (for videos)
- Scrapbooking materials
- Materials for bulletin board display
- Large blank lined index cards (for instruction cards)
- Holiday lights (for quiz boards)
- Aluminum foil (for quiz boards)
- Wires (for quiz boards)

Special Notes on the Use of This Menu

- This menu gives students the opportunity to create an informational video. The grading and sharing of these products can often be facilitated by having students prerecord their product using whatever technology is most convenient for the teacher. This allows the teacher to decide when it will be shown as well as keeps the presentation to its intended length. If recording options are limited, this activity can be modified by allowing students to act out the product (like a play) in front of the class.
- This menu allows students to create a bulletin board display. Some classrooms may only have one bulletin board, so the teacher can divide the board into sections, or additional classroom wall or hall

space can be sectioned off for the creation of these displays. Students can plan their display based on the amount of space they are assigned.

- This menu provides the opportunity for students to create a quiz board. There are many variations for these quiz boards. Instructional videos and written instructions are readily available online.

Time Frame

- 1–2 weeks—Students are given a menu as the unit is started, and the teacher discusses all of the product options on the menu. As the different options are discussed, students will choose the activities they are most interested in completing so that they meet their goal of 100 points. As the lessons progress through the week(s), the teacher and students refer back to the menu options associated with the content being taught.
- 1–2 days—The teacher chooses an activity or product from the menu to use with the entire class.

Suggested Forms

- All-purpose rubric
- Proposal form for point-based projects
- Presentation rubric

Circles

Directions: Choose at least two activities from the menu below. The activities must total 100 points. Place a checkmark next to each box to show which activities you will complete. All activities must be completed by _____ .

---

20 Points

- ❏ Create a poster that shows the formula of a circle with at least two different graphed examples.
- ❏ Build a quiz board that asks players to match circle formulas with their centers and radii.

---

50 Points

- ❏ Design an *original* circles worksheet that allows others to practice different ways to write circle equations. Your answer key should include step-by-step instructions.
- ❏ Write an instruction card that explains how to change a circle equation from center-radius form to general form.
- ❏ Prepare a scrapbook of photos of different sized circular items. Record an equation for the items on each page.
- ❏ **Free choice on writing the equation of a circle**—Prepare a proposal form and submit it to your teacher for approval.

---

80 Points

- ❏ Research two famous circles: Stonehenge and Place Charles de Gaulle, Paris. Using their precise locations on Earth, assemble a bulletin board display that shares each circular equation and how you calculated it.
- ❏ Record an informational video in which you visit at least six different circular shapes in your school, calculating and sharing the formulas of each.

Circle Relationships

Three-Topic List Menu

Objectives Covered Through This Menu and These Activities
- Students will identify and apply theorems about circles, including relationships among angles, radii, chords, tangents, and secants.
- Students will communicate mathematical ideas, reasoning, and their implications using multiple representations.
- Students will create and use representations to organize, record, and communicate mathematical ideas.
- Students will display, explain, and justify mathematical ideas and arguments using precise mathematical language in written or oral communication.

Materials Needed by Students for Completion
- Poster board or large white paper
- Microsoft PowerPoint or other slideshow software
- Blank index cards (for trading cards, concentration cards)
- Recording software or application (for videos)
- Graph paper or Internet access (for WebQuests)
- Recycled materials (for museum exhibits)
- Holiday lights (for quiz boards)
- Aluminum foil (for quiz boards)
- Wires (for quiz boards)

Special Notes on the Use of This Menu
- This menu gives students the opportunity to create a video. The grading and sharing of these products can often be facilitated by having students prerecord their product using whatever technology is most convenient for the teacher. This allows the teacher to decide when it will be shown as well as keeps the presentation to its intended length. If recording options are limited, this activity can be modified by allowing students to act out the product (like a play) in front of the class.
- This menu asks students to use recycled materials to create their museum exhibit. This does not mean only plastic and paper; instead, students should focus on using materials in new ways. It works well if a box is started for "recycled" contributions at the beginning of the

school year. That way, students always have access to these types of materials.

- This menu gives students the opportunity to facilitate a class game. The expectation is that all students in the classroom will play an active role in the game. This may mean that students need some additional space and time for their game. This can take a significant amount of time and organization. It can save time if all of the students who choose to present their game can sign up for a designated day and time that is determined when the menu is distributed.

- This menu provides the opportunity for students to create a quiz board. There are many variations for these quiz boards. Instructional videos and written instructions are readily available online.

- This menu allows students to create a WebQuest. There are multiple versions and templates for WebQuests available on the Internet. It is your decision whether you would like to specify a format or if you will allow students to create one of their own choosing.

Time Frame

- 1–2 weeks—Students are given the menu as the unit is started, and the guidelines and point expectations are discussed. Students usually will need to earn 100 points for 100%, although there is an opportunity for extra credit if the teacher would like to use another target number. Because this menu covers one topic in depth, the teacher will go over all of the options for the topic being covered and have students place checkmarks in the boxes next to the activities they are most interested in completing. Teachers will need to set aside a few moments to sign the agreement at the bottom of the page with each student. As instruction continues, activities are completed by students and submitted to the teacher for grading.

- 1–2 days—The teacher chooses an activity or product from an objective to use with the entire class during that lesson time.

Suggested Forms

- All-purpose rubric
- Proposal form for point-based products
- Presentation rubric

Name:_____ Date:_____

Circle Relationships

Guidelines:

1. You may complete as many of the activities listed as you wish within the time period.
2. You may choose any combination of activities, but **must** complete at least one activity from each topic area.
3. Your goal is 100 points. (This is a grade of 100/100.) You may earn up to _____ points extra credit.
4. You may be as creative as you like within the guidelines listed below.
5. You must show your plan to your teacher by _____ .
6. Activities may be turned in at any time during the working time period. They will be graded and recorded on this sheet as you continue to work, so keep it safe!

Topic	Plan to Do	Activity to Complete	Point Value	Date Completed	Points Earned
Properties of Circles		Create a window pane with labeled drawings for all of the circle line segments discussed in class.	10		
		Assemble a set of three-way concentration cards that allow users to match names, drawings, and definitions for the specific line segments associated with circles.	15		
		Design a set of trading cards for the different line segments related to circles. Your cards should also include theorems that may be associated with each.	20		
		Draw a Venn diagram to compare the different types of line segments we identify and calculate in a circle.	25		
		The chord of a circle has decided it should be the president of the Line Segment Association for a certain circle because it is represented most. Secant feels that it is the rightful choice. Record a speech in which the chord or secant states its position and reasoning.	30		
Circle Theorems		On a poster, make a chart noting each of the circle relationships and associated theorems for each.	10		
		Build a quiz board in which users will match circle segments with associated theorems.	15		
		Write Three Facts and Fib about using chords to calculate arc lengths.	20		
		Design a museum exhibit that could be used to teach museum visitors about the different theorems that can be used to show circle relationships.	25		
		Consider the circle theorems we are studying. Record a video in which you share how at least three of the theorems depend on each other. Use examples to support your views.	30		

Name:_____ Date:_____

Circle Relationships, continued

Topic	Plan to Do	Activity to Complete	Point Value	Date Completed	Points Earned
Using Circle Theorems		Write an original worksheet (with answer key) that has others calculating measurements given various secant, tangent, and chord lengths.	15		
		Create a class game in which teams work to use circle theorems to solve original geometry problems.	20		
		Chords are often used in word problems to determine distances across circular landmarks. Research these types of problems and prepare a PowerPoint that shares how to approach these problems.	25		
		Consider all of the theorems associated with circles. Design a WebQuest that allows questors to explore the theorem you believe is the foundation for the others.	30		
Any		**Free Choice:** Submit your free-choice proposal form for a product of your choice.			
		Total number of points you are planning to earn.	**Total points earned:**		

I am planning to complete _____ activities that could earn up to a total of _____ points.

Teacher's initials _____ Student's signature _____

Arc Length and Sector Area

Meal Menu

Objectives Covered Through This Menu and These Activities
- Students will apply the proportional relationship between the measure of an arc length of a circle and the circumference of the circle to solve problems.
- Students will apply the proportional relationship between the measure of the area of a sector of a circle and the area of the circle to solve problems.
- Students will apply mathematics to problems found in everyday life.
- Students will use problem-solving models to address real-world problems.
- Students will communicate mathematical ideas, reasoning, and their implications using multiple representations.
- Students will create and use representations to organize, record, and communicate mathematical ideas.
- Students will analyze mathematical relationships to connect and communicate mathematical ideas.
- Students will display, explain, and justify mathematical ideas and arguments using precise mathematical language in written or oral communication.

Materials Needed by Students for Completion
- Poster board or large white paper
- Materials for board games (folders, colored cards, etc.)
- Microsoft PowerPoint or other slideshow software
- Recording software or application (for videos)
- Materials for bulletin board display
- Large blank lined index cards (for instruction cards)
- Method for recording responses to word problems

Special Notes on the Use of This Menu
- This menu is a product and problem menu; it asks students to not only create products to demonstrate their knowledge but also answer one or more higher-level word problems. It is set up in such a way that students will have to complete at least one of the word problems.

When introducing this menu, teachers will need to have already determined how they would like these problems completed and recorded for grading. Remember, this is the opportunity to hold high standards when it comes to showing work and defending answers!

- This menu gives students the opportunity to create a video. The grading and sharing of these products can often be facilitated by having students prerecord their product using whatever technology is most convenient for the teacher. This allows the teacher to decide when it will be shown as well as keeps the presentation to its intended length. If recording options are limited, this activity can be modified by allowing students to act out the product (like a play) in front of the class.
- This menu gives students the opportunity to teach a concept. This can take a significant amount of time and organization. It can save time if the students who choose to do a lesson can sign up for a designated day and time that is determined when the menu is distributed.
- This menu allows students to create a bulletin board display. Some classrooms may only have one bulletin board, so the teacher can divide the board into sections, or additional classroom wall or hall space can be sectioned off for the creation of these displays. Students can plan their display based on the amount of space they are assigned.

Time Frame

- 2–3 weeks—Students are given the menu as the unit is started. As the lesson or unit progresses throughout the week, students should refer back to the menu options associated with that content. The teacher will go over all of the options for that objective and have students place a checkmark in the box for each option that represents the activity they are most interested in completing. As teaching continues, the activities chosen and completed should create a full day's meal, with a breakfast, a lunch, a dinner, and an optional dessert. The teacher may choose to allow students time to work after other work is finished. When students complete the menu with this expectation, they have completed one activity from each content area, learning style, or level of Bloom's revised taxonomy, depending on the design of the menu.
- 1 week—At the start of the unit, the teacher chooses one activity from each meal family he or she feels is most valuable for students. Stations can be set up in the classroom. These three activities are available for student choice throughout the week as regular instruction takes place.

- 1–2 days—The teacher chooses an activity or product from an objective to use with the entire class during that lesson time. Additionally, the teacher could choose one of the two desserts as an enrichment activity.

Suggested Forms

- All-purpose rubric
- Student-taught lesson rubric
- Free-choice proposal form
- Presentation rubric

Answers to Menu Problems

Problem 1: Industrial sprinklers have been installed in the two corners of your school's yard. If each sprinkler can spray everything within 7 m, and the sprinkler is set to cover 60°, how much area will the sprinklers cover?

$$A_{sector} = \frac{angle}{whole\ circle} = \frac{A_{sector}}{Total\ area\ \left(\pi r^2\right)}$$

$$\frac{60°}{360°} = \frac{A_{sector}}{\pi\left(7\ m\right)^2}$$

$$\frac{1}{6} = \frac{A_{sector}}{153.9\ m^2}$$

$$\frac{152.9\ m^2}{6} = A_{sector}$$

$$25.66\ m^2 = A_{sector}$$

Each sprinkler will cover 25.66 m², so the sprinklers will cover 51.32 m² in total.

Problem 2: A 25 ft extension ladder was leaned against a wall at angle of elevation of 87°. If the person standing on the top of the ladder accidentally pushed away from the wall and the ladder fell backward to the ground, how far did the person fall?

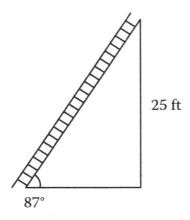

25 ft

87°

The ladder is going to fall for 93° (180° − 87°).

$$\frac{part}{360°} = \frac{arc\ length}{total\ length}$$

$$\frac{93°}{360°} = \frac{arc\ length}{2\pi r}$$

$$\frac{31°}{120°} = \frac{arc\ length}{2\pi(25)}$$

$$157.1\ ft \left[\frac{31°}{120°} = \frac{arc\ length}{157.1\ ft}\right] 157.1\ ft$$

$$40.6\ ft = arc\ length$$

The person will fall a length of 40.6 ft.

Problem 3: A farmer has installed a feeding system in which a dispenser is installed on one wall of the 20 ft² barn. If the feeder has a radius of 15 ft and is set to rotate at 100°, and it sprays 150 g of feed with each cycle, what percent of the barn will receive feed?

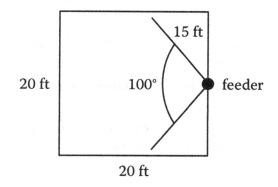

Total area of barn = lw

$$A = 20 \text{ ft } (20 \text{ ft})$$

$$A = 400 \text{ ft}^2$$

$$\frac{\text{part}}{360°} = \frac{\text{sector area}}{\text{total area}}$$

$$\frac{100°}{360°} = \frac{\text{sector area}}{\pi r^2}$$

$$\frac{100°}{360°} = \frac{\text{sector area}}{\pi \left(15 \text{ ft}\right)^2}$$

$$706.86 \text{ ft}^2 \left[\frac{5}{18} = \frac{\text{sector area}}{706.86 \text{ ft}^2}\right] 706.86 \text{ ft}^2$$

$$196.3 \text{ ft}^2 = \text{sector area}$$

$$\text{Percent} = \frac{\text{part}}{\text{whole}}\left(100\right)$$

$$\text{Percent} = \frac{196.3 \text{ ft}^2}{400 \text{ ft}^2}\left(100\right)$$

$$\text{Percent} = 49.1\%$$

The feeder will cover about 49.1% of the barn.

Arc Length and Sector Area

Directions: Choose one activity each for breakfast, lunch, and dinner. Dessert is an activity you can choose to do after you have finished your other meals. All products must be completed by: _____ .

Breakfast

- ❏ Write an instruction card that explains how to calculate the radius when given the sector area and central angle.

- ❏ Assemble a bulletin board display that shares at least four real-world examples of sector area and arc length.

- ❏ Write and perform an original song or rap that teaches others about measurements needed to calculate the area of sector in a circle.

Lunch

- ❏ Investigate the radius and coverage angles of at least three different brands of circular sprinklers, that do not rotate 360°. Prepare a PowerPoint presentation to share information about each brand and determine which sprinkler will cover the greatest area.

- ❏ Record a video to share how to calculate the sector area of various circular figures in the world around us.

- ❏ Prepare a worksheet to help others choose between different sized slices of circular food with the purpose of getting the most!

Dinner

- ❏ **Problem 1:** Industrial sprinklers have been installed in the two corners of your school's yard. If each sprinkler can spray everything within 7 m, and the sprinkler is set to cover 60°, how much area will the sprinklers cover?

- ❏ **Problem 2:** A 25 ft extension ladder was leaned against a wall at angle of elevation of 87°. If the person standing on the top of the ladder accidentally pushed away from wall and the ladder fell backwards to the ground, how far did the person fall?

- ❏ **Problem 3:** A farmer has installed a feeding system in which a dispenser is installed on one wall of the 20 ft^2 barn. If the feeder has a radius of 15 ft and is set to rotate at 100°, and it sprays 150 g of feed with each cycle, what percent of the barn will receive feed?

Dessert

- ❏ **Free choice on calculating arc length and sector area**—Prepare a proposal form and submit it to your teacher for approval.

- ❏ Record a class lesson to teach others about the relationship between the radians and a circle's arc lengths and sector areas.

CHAPTER 9

Logic, Constructions, and Probability

Logic Statements

Tic-Tac-Toe Menu

Objectives Covered Through This Menu and These Activities

- Students will identify and determine the validity of the converse, inverse, and contrapositive of a conditional statement and recognize the connection between a biconditional statement and a true conditional statement with a true converse.
- Students will communicate mathematical ideas, reasoning, and their implications using multiple representations.
- Students will create and use representations to organize, record, and communicate mathematical ideas.
- Students will display, explain, and justify mathematical ideas and arguments using precise mathematical language in written or oral communication.

Materials Needed by Students for Completion

- Poster board or large white paper
- Materials for board games (folders, colored cards, etc.)
- Recording software or application (for videos)
- Materials for bulletin board display
- Large blank lined index cards (for instruction cards)

Special Notes on the Use of This Menu

- This menu gives students the opportunity to create a video. The grading and sharing of these products can often be facilitated by having students prerecord their product using whatever technology is most convenient for the teacher. This allows the teacher to decide when it will be shown as well as keeps the presentation to its intended length. If recording options are limited, this activity can be modified by allowing students to act out the product (like a play) in front of the class.
- This menu gives students the opportunity to teach a concept. This can take a significant amount of time and organization. It can save time if the students who choose to do a lesson can sign up for a designated day and time that is determined when the menu is distributed.
- This menu allows students to create a bulletin board display. Some classrooms may only have one bulletin board, so the teacher can

divide the board into sections, or additional classroom wall or hall space can be sectioned off for the creation of these displays. Students can plan their display based on the amount of space they are assigned.

Time Frame

- 2–3 weeks—Students are given the menu as the unit is started. The teacher will go over all of the options for that content and have students place checkmarks in the boxes that represent the activities they are most interested in completing. As students choose activities, they should complete a column or a row. When students complete this pattern, they have completed one activity from each content area, learning style, or level of Bloom's revised taxonomy, depending on the design of the menu. As the teacher presents lessons throughout the week, he or she should refer back to the menu options associated with that content.
- 1 week—At the start of the unit, the teacher chooses the three activities he or she feels are most valuable for students. Stations can be set up in the classroom. These three activities are available for student choice throughout the week as regular instruction takes place.
- 1–2 days—The teacher chooses an activity from the menu to use with the entire class.

Suggested Forms

- All-purpose rubric
- Student-taught lesson rubric
- Free-choice proposal form
- Presentation rubric

Logic Statements

Directions: Check the boxes you plan to complete. They should form a tic-tac-toe across or down. All products are due by: _____ .

☐ *Writing Logic Statements* Record an instructional video in which you share how to write logic statements based on real-world events.	☐ *Validity of Logic Statements* Write Three Facts and a Fib about a specific biconditional statement and the validity of its converse and contrapositive.	☐ *Logic Statements in Geometry* Create a worksheet to help others practice writing different forms of geometric conditional statements.
☐ *Logic Statements in Geometry* Create a "Logic Statements in Geometry" brochure that shares different geometric theorems and their inverses, converses, and contrapositives.	☐ **Free Choice: Writing Logic Statements** (Fill out your proposal form before beginning the free choice!)	☐ *Validity of Logic Statements* Write and perform an original song that shows how inverses, converses, and contrapositives can be funny compared to the original conditional statement.
☐ *Validity of Logic Statements* Prepare a bulletin board display that shows how to assess the validity of the converse, inverse, and contrapositive of a conditional statement.	☐ *Logic Statements in Geometry* Record a student-taught lesson on the use and importance of logic statements in geometry.	☐ *Writing Logic Statements* Write an instruction card that explains how to write and evaluate the inverse, converse, and contrapositive of a conditional statement.

Combinations and Permutations

Tic-Tac-Toe Menu

Objectives Covered Through This Menu and These Activities

- Students will develop strategies to use permutations and combinations to solve contextual problems.
- Students will determine probabilities based on area to solve contextual problems.
- Students will identify whether two events are independent and compute the probability of the two events occurring together with or without replacement.
- Students will apply conditional probability in contextual problems.
- Students will apply mathematics to problems found in everyday life.
- Students will use problem-solving models to address real-world problems.
- Students will communicate mathematical ideas, reasoning, and their implications using multiple representations.
- Students will analyze mathematical relationships to connect and communicate mathematical ideas.
- Students will display, explain, and justify mathematical ideas and arguments using precise mathematical language in written or oral communication.

Materials Needed by Students for Completion

- Poster board or large white paper
- Microsoft PowerPoint or other slideshow software
- Blank index cards (for trading cards, concentration cards)
- Recording software or application (for videos)
- Scrapbooking materials
- Recycled materials (for models)

Special Notes on the Use of This Menu

- This menu gives students the opportunity to create a video. The grading and sharing of these products can often be facilitated by having students prerecord their product using whatever technology is most convenient for the teacher. This allows the teacher to decide when it will be shown as well as keeps the presentation to its intended length.

If recording options are limited, this activity can be modified by allowing students to act out the product (like a play) in front of the class.
- This menu asks students to use recycled materials to create their models. This does not mean only plastic and paper; instead, students should focus on using materials in new ways. It works well if a box is started for "recycled" contributions at the beginning of the school year. That way, students always have access to these types of materials.

Time Frame
- 2–3 weeks—Students are given the menu as the unit is started. The teacher will go over all of the options for that content and have students place checkmarks in the boxes that represent the activities they are most interested in completing. As students choose activities, they should complete a column or a row. When students complete this pattern, they have completed one activity from each content area, learning style, or level of Bloom's revised taxonomy, depending on the design of the menu. As the teacher presents lessons throughout the week, he or she should refer back to the menu options associated with that content.
- 1 week—At the start of the unit, the teacher chooses the three activities he or she feels are most valuable for students. Stations can be set up in the classroom. These three activities are available for student choice throughout the week as regular instruction takes place.
- 1–2 days—The teacher chooses an activity from the menu to use with the entire class.

Suggested Forms
- All-purpose rubric
- Free-choice proposal form
- Presentation rubric

Combinations and Permutations

Directions: Check the boxes you plan to complete. They should form a tic-tac-toe across or down. All products are due by: _____ .

☐ *Combinations or Permutations* Assemble a scrapbook of real-world probability situations. On each page indicate if each is a combination or permutation as well as a word problem with a solution that could accompany it.	☐ *Will It or Won't It?* Your booster club has decided to play Cow Pie Bingo to raise funds. If your football field area is divided into equal squares, and you buy two squares, record a video to share the probability that you will win the bingo. (*Note:* You will have to do some research to answer this!)	☐ *Multiple Events* Create an original worksheet (and answer key) to help your classmates practice identifying and solving real-world problems with independent and dependent events. Your worksheet must be original, including problems not found on the Internet.
☐ *Multiple Events* Make a set of trading cards for different real-world independent and dependent events. Your cards should include at least one sample word problem with an answer for each event.	☐ **Free Choice: Combinations or Permutations** (Fill out your proposal form before beginning the free choice!)	☐ *Will It or Won't It?* Carnivals offer lots of different games on the midway, but most are very difficult to win based on probability. Build two different models of carnival games with calculations explaining why they are so difficult to win.
☐ *Will It or Won't It?* Investigate the strategies that professional baseball players use to reduce the area of the strike zone and present a PowerPoint presentation that shows the probability of hitting the strike zone for a taller or a shorter player.	☐ *Multiple Events* Write a who-done-it mystery play or children's book in which the audience is required to use the probability of independent and dependent events in the storyline to solve the mystery.	☐ *Combinations or Permutations* Prepare a set of concentration cards in which players match real-world probability problems with the combination or permutation solution that should accompany each.

```
┌──┬──┬──┐
├──┼──┼──┤
├──┼──┼──┤
└──┴──┴──┘
```

Constructions

Tic-Tac-Toe Menu

Objectives Covered Through This Menu and These Activities

- Students will construct various geometric constructions, such as congruent segments, congruent angles, a segment bisector, an angle bisector, perpendicular lines, the perpendicular bisector of a line segment, and a line parallel to a given line through a point not on a line using a compass and a straightedge.
- Students will use constructions to make conjectures about geometric relationships.
- Students will analyze mathematical relationships to connect and communicate mathematical ideas.
- Students will display, explain, and justify mathematical ideas and arguments using precise mathematical language in written or oral communication.

Materials Needed by Students for Completion

- Poster board or large white paper
- Microsoft PowerPoint or other slideshow software
- Blank index cards (for trading cards)
- Recording software or application (for videos)
- Ruler (for comic strips)
- Scrapbooking materials
- Materials for bulletin board display

Special Notes on the Use of This Menu

- This menu gives students the opportunity to create a video. The grading and sharing of these products can often be facilitated by having students prerecord their product using whatever technology is most convenient for the teacher. This allows the teacher to decide when it will be shown as well as keeps the presentation to its intended length. If recording options are limited, this activity can be modified by allowing students to act out the product (like a play) in front of the class.
- This menu gives students the opportunity to facilitate a class game. The expectation is that all students in the classroom will play an active role in the game. This may mean that the facilitator may need some

additional space and time for his or her game. This can take a significant amount of time and organization. It can save time if all of the students who choose to present their game can sign up for a designated day and time that is determined when the menu is distributed.

- This menu allows students to create a bulletin board display. Some classrooms may only have one bulletin board, so the teacher can divide the board into sections, or additional classroom wall or hall space can be sectioned off for the creation of these displays. Students can plan their display based on the amount of space they are assigned.

Time Frame

- 2–3 weeks—Students are given the menu as the unit is started. The teacher will go over all of the options for that content and have students place checkmarks in the boxes that represent the activities they are most interested in completing. As students choose activities, they should complete a column or a row. When students complete this pattern, they have completed one activity from each content area, learning style, or level of Bloom's revised taxonomy, depending on the design of the menu. As the teacher presents lessons throughout the week, he or she should refer back to the menu options associated with that content.
- 1 week—At the start of the unit, the teacher chooses the three activities he or she feels are most valuable for students. Stations can be set up in the classroom. These three activities are available for student choice throughout the week as regular instruction takes place.
- 1–2 days—The teacher chooses an activity from the menu to use with the entire class.

Suggested Forms

- All-purpose rubric
- Free-choice proposal form
- Presentation rubric

Name:_____ Date:_____

Constructions

Directions: Check the boxes you plan to complete. They should form a tic-tac-toe across or down. All products are due by: _____ .

You must use each of these constructions at least once while completing this menu:

☐ _____   ☐ _____   ☐ _____

☐ _____   ☐ _____   ☐ _____

☐ _____   ☐ _____   ☐ _____

☐ *Teaching Constructions*	☐ *Constructions*	☐ *Using Constructions*
Record an instruction video that could be uploaded to YouTube to teach middle school students how to construct various geometric concepts.	Make a set of trading cards for each construction. Each card should include information about the construction, how to complete it, and what theorems are associated with it.	You have been hired to create a logo for a company that publishes geometry materials. Using an online drawing tool, create a PowerPoint slide with a logo created from geometric constructions.
☐ *Using Constructions*	☐ **Free Choice: Teaching Constructions** (Fill out your proposal form before beginning the free choice!)	☐ *Constructions*
Draw a comic strip or cartoon in which each character is created from a geometric construction.		Design a cooperative class game in which teams answer questions about and work together to show different geometric constructions.
☐ *Constructions*	☐ *Using Constructions*	☐ *Teaching Constructions*
Assemble a constructions scrapbook with each page dedicated to a different construction, how it is made, and its importance in geometry.	On a poster, create a piece of artwork from at least five different geometric constructions.	Build an interactive bulletin board display that teaches others how to use math tools to construct at least two geometric concepts.

References

Anderson, L., & Krathwohl, D. R. (Eds.). (2001). *A taxonomy for learning, teaching, and assessing: A revision of Bloom's taxonomy of educational objectives* (Complete ed.). New York, NY: Longman.

Deci, E. L., Vallerand, R. J., Pelletier, L. G., & Ryan, R. M. (1991). Motivation and education: The self-determination perspective. *Educational Psychologist, 26,* 325–346.

Dunn, R., & Honigsfeld, A. (2013). Learning styles: What we know and what we need. *The Educational Forum, 77,* 225–232. doi:10.1080/00131725.2013.765328

Flowerday, T., & Schraw, G. (2003). Effect of choice on cognitive and affective engagement. *The Journal of Educational Research, 96,* 207–215. doi:10.1080/00220670309598810

Keen, D. (2001). *Talent in the new millennium: Report on year one of the programme.* Paper presented at the meeting of the Australian Association for Research in Education, Perth.

Komarraju, M., Karau, S. J., Schmeck, R. R., & Avdic, A. (2011). The Big Five personality traits, learning styles, and academic achievement. *Personality and Individual Differences, 51,* 472–477. http://dx.doi.org/10.1016/j.paid.2011.04.019

Litman, J. (2005). Epistemic curiosity, feeling-of-knowing, and exploratory behaviour. *Cognition & Emotion, 19,* 559–582.

Magner, L. (2000). Reaching all children through differentiated assessment: The 2-5-8 plan. *Gifted Child Today, 23*(3), 48–50.

Patall, E. A. (2013). Constructing motivation through choice, interest, and interestingness. *Journal of Educational Psychology, 105,* 522–534. doi:10.1037/a0030307

Ricca, J. (1984). Learning styles and preferred instructional strategies of gifted students. *Gifted Child Quarterly, 28,* 121–126.

Robinson, J., Patall, E. A., & Cooper, H. (2008). The effects of choice on intrinsic motivation and related outcomes: a meta-analysis of research findings. *Psychological Bulletin, 134,* 270–300.

Sagan, L. (2010). Students' choice: Recommendations for environmental and instructional changes in school. *The Clearing House: A Journal of Educational Strategies, Issues and Ideas, 83,* 217–222. doi:10.1080/00098650903505407

Snyder, R. (1999). The relationship between learning styles/multiple intelligences and academic achievement of high school students. *The High School Journal, 83*(2), 11–20.

About the Author

After teaching science for more than 15 years, both overseas and in the U.S., **Laurie E. Westphal, Ed.D.,** now works as an independent gifted education and science consultant nationwide. She enjoys developing and presenting staff development on low-stress differentiation strategies and using menus for various districts and conferences, working with teachers to assist them in planning and developing lessons to meet the needs of their advanced students. Laurie currently resides in Houston, TX, and has made it her goal to convert as many teachers as she can to the differentiated lifestyle in the classroom and to share her vision for real-world, product-based lessons that help all students become critical thinkers and effective problem solvers. She is the author of the Differentiating Instruction With Menus series as well as *Hands-On Physical Science* and *Science Dictionary for Kids.*

Common Core State Standards Alignment

This book aligns with an extensive number of the Common Core State Standards. Please visit https://www.prufrock.com/ccss.aspx to download a complete packet of the standards that align with each individual menu in this book.